D0252113

The Oxford French dictionary range also includes the following:

The Oxford–Hachette French Dictionary
The Concise Oxford–Hachette French Dictionary
The Compact Oxford–Hachette French Dictionary
The Oxford Paperback French Dictionary
The Oxford Paperback French Dictionary and Grammar
The Oxford French Minidictionary
French Grammar
10,000 French Words
French Verbs
The Oxford–Duden Pictorial French Dictionary, Second Edition

French Usage

Richard Wakely
and Henri Béjoint

Oxford   New York
OXFORD UNIVERSITY PRESS
1996

Oxford University Press, Walton Street, Oxford OX2 6DP

Oxford New York
Athens Auckland Bangkok Bogota Bombay
Buenos Aires Calcutta Cape Town Dar es Salaam
Delhi Florence Hong Kong Istanbul Karachi
Kuala Lumpur Madras Madrid Melbourne
Mexico City Nairobi Paris Singapore
Taipei Tokyo Toronto
and associated companies in
Berlin Ibadan

Oxford is a trade mark of Oxford University Press

British Library Cataloguing in Publication Data
Data available

Library of Congress Cataloging in Publication Data
Data available

ISBN 0-19-864334-9

10 9 8 7 6 5 4 3 2 1

Typeset by Oxuniprint
Printed in Great Britain by
Mackays of Chatham
Chatham, Kent

Contents

Introduction

We are all familiar with the idea of grouping words according to the context in which they are used; many vocabulary books, for example, are divided into thematic sections such as *The Human Body*, *The garden*, *In a factory*, etc. The words contained in such sections are connected in the sense that they refer to things that belong to the same area of human experience.

This book also considers *families* of words, but the groupings are different. The idea for this book came from observations gathered during the preparation of the *Oxford-Hachette French Dictionary*. As in other dictionary projects, it had been decided to treat certain areas of translation difficulty centrally, rather than repeat the same information for each relevant lexical item. For example, much of the information about the words for the different days of the week is common to all of them, and can therefore be given in one place only (e.g. at the entry for *Monday*), all the other entries for the other names of days having only cross-references.

This has been common practice in many dictionaries for such *closed sets*, that is well-defined groups of a few clearly connected words. The information is generally given at one entry, selected more or less arbitrarily, as in the case of *Monday* for the days of the week, thus saving space for other information, and showing that the information is common to all the relevant entries.

The originality of the *Oxford-Hachette French Dictionary* was that special boxes were introduced, in which the information was placed within the A-Z dictionary text. These boxes were called *Usage Notes*. In addition, it soon became apparent that many more words could be treated in the same way, because they belong to groups of words that are used in similar ways, in similar constructions, with the same prepositions, etc.

Thus, the usage notes were extended to words which had never previously been treated in this way, particularly words belonging to sets that are sometimes referred to as *open*, because there is virtually no limit to the number of words they can contain, like the names of musical instruments, of diseases, etc.

This book takes the idea of usage notes two steps further. Firstly, as mentioned above, it extends the number of lexical sets to areas that had not been treated before, such as the names of animals, of flowers, of foodstuffs, etc., and, secondly, it explains in greater detail all the morphological and grammatical similarities - as well as differences - between the different words that belong to each group.

For each point of grammar or usage, examples are given of usage which can simply and straightforwardly be applied to all the other items in the set. When some members of the group have characteristics that are not shared by the other members, this is also mentioned explicitly. For example, some names of colours have corresponding verbs ending in *-ir*, meaning *to go/turn + COLOUR*, such as *blanchir*, *rougir*, *noircir*, etc. But other words for colours, such as *gris*, *marron*, etc., have no such corresponding verbs. No attempt is made to explain such phenomena in this book: they are just features of usage that the language learner must know.

The usage notes are aimed principally at the *encoder*, that is the person working from his/her native language and trying to produce *text*, oral or written, in the foreign language. In this case, the user is a native English speaker learning French. That is why the language used for all explanations is English.

This book makes use of a database of French texts (a corpus), which gives authenticity to a large number of the translations. They are in *real* French as it is used in spontaneous conversation, in newspapers, on television, on radio, etc. On the whole an effort has been made to use only the most natural expressions in French, and to avoid the stilted, unnatural sounding language that is sometimes found in books for language learners.

As we have seen at the beginning of this introduction, the first impetus for usage notes was economy of space. However, as we moved away from the small number of closed lexical sets traditionally considered in dictionaries, it soon became apparent that such groupings could also be a powerful means of boosting the learning of the words of a foreign language. Studying the contents of a usage note you will not only learn how to use one word, you will also learn how to use many others - the exact number depending on the size and homogeneity of the lexical set. Thus the book should help you to acquire vocabulary more effectively and more easily. While a grammar book deals with sentence patterns and a dictionary deals with the idiosyncrasies of each individual word, this book will help you see more clearly the relations between certain sentence patterns and certain types of words.

An effort has been made to make the book as useful as possible by:

- dividing each note into clearly marked sub-sections, so that minor points of information can be found easily
- using clear non-technical language for the explanations
- making use of an extensive system of cross-references
- making the examples as close to real usage as possible.

There are innumerable sets of words that could have been included, but we selected only those that presented real difficulties for the learner, and a reasonable number of regularities. Also, more could have been said about each set, but you will find here all the essential facts about the selected sets, and no unnecessary fine-grained niceties that would have distracted you from what is essential. We believe that

Time

Days of the week

Forms and spelling

In French it is usual to list the days of the week as
follows, with Monday first:

Monday	= **lundi**
Tuesday	= **mardi**
Wednesday	= **mercredi**
Thursday	= **jeudi**
Friday	= **vendredi**
Saturday	= **samedi**
Sunday	= **dimanche**

French does not normally use capital letters for days of
the week:

Thursday May 5th 1996	= **jeudi 5 mai 1996** (*e.g. in a letter heading*)
it was a Friday	= **c'était un vendredi**

French does not abbreviate the names of days of the
week, except on calendars (see next page), in diaries, etc.

Wed. Feb. 9th	= **mercredi 9 février**

What day?
Questions

The basic question and answer about days of the week
would go as follows:

1999

	JANVIER	FEVRIER	MARS	AVRIL	
L	3 10 17 24 31	7 14 21 28	7 14 21 28	4 11 18 25	L
M	4 11 18 25	1 8 15 22	1 8 15 22 29	5 12 19 26	M
M	5 12 19 26	2 9 16 23	2 9 16 23 30	6 13 20 27	M
J	6 13 20 27	3 10 17 24	3 10 17 24 31	7 14 21 28	J
V	7 14 21 28	4 11 18 25	4 11 18 25	1 8 15 22 29	V
S	1 8 15 22 29	5 12 19 26	5 12 19 26	2 9 16 23 30	S
D	2 9 16 23 30	6 13 20 27	6 13 20 27	3 10 17 24	D

	MAI	JUIN	JUILLET	AOUT	
L	2 9 16 23 30	6 13 20 27	4 11 18 25	1 8 15 22 29	L
M	3 10 17 24 31	7 14 21 28	5 12 19 26	2 9 16 23 30	M
M	4 11 18 25	1 8 15 22 29	6 13 20 27	3 10 17 24 31	M
J	5 12 19 26	2 9 16 23 30	7 14 21 28	4 11 18 25	J
V	6 13 20 27	3 10 17 24	1 8 15 22 29	5 12 19 26	V
S	7 14 21 28	4 11 18 25	2 9 16 23 30	6 13 20 27	S
D	1 8 15 22 29	5 12 19 26	3 10 17 24 31	7 14 21 28	D

	SEPTEMBRE	OCTOBRE	NOVEMBRE	DECEMBRE	
L	6 13 20 27	4 11 18 25	1 8 15 22 29	6 13 20 27	L
M	7 14 21 28	5 12 19 26	2 9 16 23 30	7 14 21 28	M
M	1 8 15 22 29	6 13 20 27	3 10 17 24	1 8 15 22 29	M
J	2 9 16 23 30	7 14 21 28	4 11 18 25	2 9 16 23 30	J
V	3 10 17 24	1 8 15 22 29	5 12 19 26	3 10 17 24 31	V
S	4 11 18 25	2 9 16 23 30	6 13 20 27	4 11 18 25	S
D	5 12 19 26	3 10 17 24 31	7 14 21 28	5 12 19 26	D

• Les zones colorées correspondent à des jours fériés.

what day is it (today)?   = **quel jour sommes-nous?**

it's Tuesday   = **nous sommes mardi**

In the following questions, **jour**, just like *day*, means *day of the week* rather than *date* or any other sense:

which is your day off?   = **quel est votre jour libre?**

which days (of the week)   = **elle travaille quels jours (de la**
does she work?   **semaine)?** (*colloquial*)

which day did he say   = **il a dit qu'il arrivait quel jour?**
he was coming?   (*colloquial*)

Talking about days

French does not have an equivalent for *on* when referring to a single event:

I'm seeing her on Saturday	= **je la verrai samedi**
on Monday (*i.e. next Monday*) I'm taking the car	= **lundi je prends la voiture**
they rang late on Tuesday	= **ils ont appelé mardi soir tard**
he's meeting us on Friday morning	= **il vient nous voir vendredi matin**

But when referring to a regular habit or pattern use the definite article:

on Mondays I take the car	= **le lundi je prends la voiture**
we have meetings on Friday mornings	= **on se réunit le vendredi matin**
there are matches on Saturday afternoons	= **il y a des matchs le samedi après-midi**
they used to ring late on Tuesdays	= **ils appelaient le mardi soir tard**

So:

Single events: English uses the singular; French uses no article and the noun in the singular.

Regular occurrences: English uses the plural; French uses the definite article with the noun in the singular.

This type of opposition also applies to compound phrases:

there was an article on her in Sunday's paper	= **il y avait un article sur elle dans le journal de dimanche** or **de ce dimanche**
I never get through the Sunday papers	= **je ne lis jamais les journaux du dimanche jusqu'au bout**

Saturday's performance was a success	=	**la représentation de (ce) samedi a été un succès**
we avoid the Saturday performances	=	**nous évitons les représentations du samedi**

Here are some more examples showing the difference between **regular occurrences** and **specific events**:

REGULAR OCCURRENCES

Note that the plural is used in some of the examples, and not only **le** with the singular:

we're paid every Friday	=	**on est payé tous les vendredis** or **on est payé le vendredi**
she has to go to Aberdeen every other Monday	=	**elle doit se rendre à Aberdeen un lundi sur deux**
every fourth Sunday there is a market	=	**il y a le marché un dimanche sur quatre**
each Friday the office is empty after the lunch hour	=	**tous les vendredis le bureau est vide après l'heure du déjeuner**
how come he's missing the odd Wednesday?	=	**comment ça se fait qu'il s'absente le mercredi de temps en temps?**
there's a new employee most Mondays	=	**il y a un nouvel employé presque tous les lundis**
I never work Thursdays	=	**je ne travaille jamais le jeudi**
some Thursdays it's hard to get hold of her	=	**certains jeudis on a du mal à la joindre**

SPECIFIC EVENTS

Note that **ce** (as opposed to **le**) can be used for specific events. **Ce** is obligatory with **-là**, but cannot be used with **prochain/dernier/en huit**.

she's interviewing him this Thursday	=	**elle va l'interviewer ce jeudi**

that Friday (*or* the Friday in question) it snowed all day	= **ce vendredi-là il a neigé toute la journée**
and of course he rang that very Tuesday	= **et bien sûr il a appelé précisément ce mardi-là**

Other expressions for the future include:

this coming Saturday there's a dance	= **samedi qui vient il y a un bal** (*colloquial*)
next Sunday we're invited to lunch	= **dimanche prochain on est invités à déjeuner**
in three months from Monday it'll be Christmas!	= **dans trois mois lundi ce sera Noël!**
in a month from last Thursday	= **dans un mois à dater de jeudi dernier**
we must have it by Friday	= **nous devons absolument le recevoir avant vendredi**
it's free from Tuesday	= **c'est libre à partir de mardi**

And the following refers to the past:

he died the Saturday before last	= **il est mort l'autre samedi**

Note the use of **huit (jours)** for a week and **quinze (jours)** for a fortnight. Note also the use of **en** for the future:

the Monday after next *or* Monday week is a holiday	= **lundi en huit est férié** (*colloquial*)
Tuesday fortnight there's a match	= **mardi en quinze il y a un match**
a week past Thursday	= **jeudi il y a huit jours** *or* **il y a huit jours jeudi**
a fortnight past Saturday	= **samedi il y a quinze jours** *or* **il y a quinze jours samedi**

Months of the year

Forms and spelling

French months are normally written with lower-case (rather than capital) letters.

January	=	**janvier**
February	=	**février**
March	=	**mars**
April	=	**avril**
May	=	**mai**
June	=	**juin**
July	=	**juillet**
August	=	**août** [*say* "oot"]
September	=	**septembre**
October	=	**octobre**
November	=	**novembre**
December	=	**décembre**

General principle: French names of months (which are all masculine) are not normally preceded by articles (**le**, **un**) or by demonstratives (**ce**, **ces**).

What/which month?

Questions

Note that often no preposition is needed in French.

what month is it?	= **quel mois sommes-nous?** *or* (*very colloquially*) **on est quel mois?**
in which month are you taking your holidays	= **vous prenez vos vacances quel mois?** (*colloquial*)
(in) what month was he born?	= **il est né quel mois?** (*colloquial*)

When translating *in*, **en** is common and **au mois de** is also a (more formal) possibility. **Dans** is impossible.

it happens in May = **cela a lieu en mai** *or* (*more formally*) **au mois de mai**

When translating *it* + verb *to be*, use **nous/on** + verb **être** + preposition:

it's August—and it's raining! = **on est en août—et il pleut!**

it was October before we realized = **on était en octobre avant que nous ne nous en rendions compte**

it will be April soon = **on sera bientôt en avril**

Being precise about which month in which year

Here the principle of avoiding articles and demonstratives with names of months is clearly shown:

this June is too soon = **en juin prochain ce sera trop tôt**

that August I lost my mother = **cette année-là en août j'ai perdu ma mère**

next March we'd better change the car = **en mars prochain il faudrait qu'on change de voiture**

in May next year = **l'an prochain en mai**

it'll have been a year come July = **cela fera un an en juillet**

the January after next = **en janvier dans deux ans**

the March before last was wet = **il y a deux ans en mars il a beaucoup plu**

Regular events applied to months

we take our holiday in May = **c'est en mai que nous prenons nos vacances**

we meet every July = **nous nous rencontrons tous les ans en juillet**

every other August they come and use our flat = **ils viennent occuper notre appartement tous les deux ans en août**

Certain moments within months

Note the use of expressions like **fin janvier** and **début juin**.
The fuller forms, such as **à la fin de janvier**, are equally
correct but more formal and thus rarer in everyday
usage.

at the beginning of March	= **début mars** or **au début du mois de mars**
at the end of January	= **fin janvier** or **à la fin du mois de janvier**
before the end of March	= **avant la fin mars** or **avant la fin du mois de mars**
in late May	= **fin mai** or **vers la fin du mois de mai**
in early June	= **début juin** or **vers le début du mois de juin**
in mid-April	= **à la mi-avril**
approved right at the beginning of March	= **approuvé dès le début mars**

With adjectives

It is safest to use **mois de**:

the warmest February on record	= **le mois de février le plus chaud qu'on ait jamais vu**
it was a really rainy June	= **c'était un mois de juin vraiment pluvieux**

from/to

à partir de is more precise than **de**; **jusque** is more precise
than **à**:

it dates from the beginning of January	= **cela date du début janvier**
there are a lot of geese from October to January	= **les oies abondent d'octobre à janvier**
the first semester (mid-October to the end of January)	= **le premier semestre (mi-octobre à fin janvier)**

from the beginning of = **à partir de début mai**
    May onwards

till the end of September = **jusqu'à fin septembre**

from June (right) = **à partir de juin et jusqu'en**
    through to December   **décembre**

Length applied to months

Again, adding the words **mois de** works best:

she worked for the = **elle a travaillé tout le mois de juin**
    whole of June   *or* **pendant tout le mois de juin**

throughout August it = **il a plu tout le mois d'août** *or*
    rained   **pendant tout le mois d'août**

Uses with other nouns

It is sometimes possible to use **de** + month:

one May morning = **un matin de mai**

that August night in = **ce soir d'août en 1949**
    1949

It is always safe to use **du mois de**:

the July flights are full = **les vols du mois de juillet sont**
    pleins

bought in the January = **acheté dans les soldes du mois de**
    sales   **janvier**

....

Seasons

Forms and spelling

the four seasons = **les quatre saisons**

French uses lower-case letters, rather than capitals. Note
that the French names for seasons are masculine:

Spring = **printemps** *m*

Summer = **été** *m*

Autumn = **automne** *m*

Winter = **hiver** *m*

What season?

When translating *in*, use **au** with **printemps** and **en** with the other words:

in Spring	= **au printemps**
in Summer/Autumn/ Winter	= **en été/en automne/en hiver**

Even when English omits *the*, French includes **le** (*or, in combination*, **du/de l', au/à l'**):

in early Summer	= **au début de l'été**
in late Spring	= **à la fin du printemps**
for the whole Winter	= **pendant tout l'hiver**
last Autumn	= **l'automne dernier**
I'll buy a new car next Spring	= **j'achèterai une voiture neuve au printemps prochain**
the Spring after next	= **dans deux ans au printemps**
last Summer we went swimming every day	= **l'été dernier nous nous sommes baignés tous les jours**

No article may be used, however, with **chaque**, **ce(t)**, or **en**:

every Summer	= **chaque été**
the Summer before last	= **il y a deux ans en été**
this Winter	= **cet hiver**
until Autumn	= **jusqu'en automne**

When translating the name of a season used as an adjective, use **de** alone, with no article:

winter clothes	= **des vêtements d'hiver**
the summer collections	= **les collections d'été**
a spring day	= **un jour de printemps**

a summer evening	= **un soir d'été**
autumn weather	= **un temps d'automne**

Compare the above with the following examples. Here, the definite article is used in French:

last Winter's clothes	= **les vêtements de l'hiver dernier**
last Summer's collections	= **les collections de l'été dernier**
a day next Spring	= **un jour du printemps prochain**

....

Dates

What's the date?

what's the date (today)?	= **quel jour sommes-nous (aujourd'hui)?**
it's the tenth	= **nous sommes** or (*more colloquial*) **on est le dix**
it's the tenth of May	= **nous sommes** or (*more colloquial*) **on est le dix mai**

See below for full forms of dates with the day of the week and the year.

Days of the week and month
Writing dates

French has only two commonly used ways of writing dates. In both, you use **1er** = **premier** for the first of the month; otherwise, use cardinal numbers (**2**, **10**, etc.). The definite article is obligatory if the day of the week is not mentioned; optional if it is.

DATES WITHOUT THE DAY OF THE WEEK
The French expression **le 10 septembre** corresponds to all of the English expressions: *September 10th; September 10; 10th September*, etc., also *Sept. 10th*, as French does

not abbreviate the names of months, except on calendars.
For a sample of calendar, see *Days of the week.*

DATES WITH THE DAY OF THE WEEK
Put the day of the week first, as in English:

Monday, September 10th	= **le lundi 10 septembre** *or* **lundi 10 septembre**

shorter version:

Monday 10th	= **lundi 10** *or* **le lundi 10**

Speaking dates

Write	Say
le 1er novembre	**le premier novembre**
le 23 juin	**le vingt-trois juin**
le lundi 31 mars	**le lundi trente-et-un mars**

More colloquially:

jeudi 15	**jeudi quinze**

On a particular day
French uses the definite article, and does not use a word
equivalent to *on:*

it happened on the sixth	= **cela s'est passé le six**
she left on November 9th	= **elle est partie le 9 novembre**
on the 2nd of every month	= **le 2 de chaque mois**
he'll be here on the 3rd	= **il sera là le trois**

Other expressions
The definite article (as usual) often combines to give the
regular forms **au** and **du:**

from the 10th onwards	= **à partir du dix**
from 21st to 30th May	= **du 21 au 30 mai**
around 16th May	= **aux environs du 16 mai**
until 21st June	= **jusqu'au 21 juin**

the newspaper of 3rd   = **le journal du 3 juin**
    June

See also *Days of the week*: **à partir de lundi 6 juin** and **à partir du lundi 6 juin** are both correct.

Years in dates

Note the two ways of saying hundreds and thousands in dates:

Write	Say
1968	**mille neuf cent soixante-huit** *or* **dix-neuf cent soixante-huit**
1723	**mille sept cent vingt-trois** *or* **dix-sept cent vingt-trois**

Everyday usage shifts as between the above ways of saying dates/years. Certain well-known dates use one rather than the other:

1515   = **quinze cent quinze**

In general, this latter way is used for dates up to the 1600s, i.e. **seize cent** rather than **mille six cent**.

BC and *AD*

Write: **av. J.-C.**   Say: **avant Jésus-Christ**

in 2500 BC   = **en 2500 avant Jésus-Christ**

Write: **apr. J.-C.**   Say: **après Jésus-Christ**

in 230 AD   = **en 230 après Jésus-Christ**

Translating *in*

French usually uses **en**:

in 1968 =   Write: **en 1968**   Say: **en mille neuf cent soixante-huit**

in 1896 =   Write: **en 1896**   Say: **en mille huit cent quatre-vingt-seize**

But use the fuller form **en l'an** for early dates, for any dates where the figure might be ambiguous, and for round thousands:

in AD 27	= **en l'an 27 après Jésus-Christ**
in 132 BC	= **en l'an 132 avant Jésus-Christ**
in the year 2000	= **en l'an 2000**

Colloquial dates

the 1912 uprising	= **le soulèvement de 1912** (*say* **mille neuf cent douze** *or* **dix-neuf cent douze**)
the 14–18 War	= **la guerre de 14–18**
May '45	= **mai '45** (*say* **mai quarante-cinq**)
the strike of '82	= **la grève de '82** (*say* **de quatre-vingt deux**)

Dates of birth and death

Shakespeare (1564–1616)	= **Shakespeare (1564–1616)** (*say* **quinze cent soixante-quatre— seize cent seize**)
Shakespeare b. 1564 d. 1616	= **Shakespeare, né en quinze cent soixante-quatre, mort en seize cent seize**

French has no abbreviations for **né** or **mort**.

Decades referred to with *-ties*

Note the use of **années** (**ans** is impossible):

the eighties	= **les années 80**
in the 70s	= **dans les années 70**
in the early 60s	= **au début des années 60**
in the late twenties	= **à la fin des années 20**

Full form of dates

she was born on Monday, 15th October 1932	= **elle est née le lundi 15 octobre 1932** (*say* **elle est née le lundi quinze octobre mille neuf cent trente-deux**)
war was declared on Sunday September 3rd 1914	= **la guerre fut déclarée le dimanche 3 septembre 1914** (*say* **la guerre fut déclarée le dimanche trois septembre mille neuf cent quatorze**)
the carnival is planned for Saturday 14th July 1996	= **le carnaval est prévu pour le samedi 14 juillet 1996** (*say* **le carnaval est prévu pour le samedi quatorze juillet mille neuf cent quatre-vingt-seize**)

Centuries

Always use the definite article in French as in English.

French normally uses Roman numerals for centuries:

the 16th Century = **le XVIe siècle**	Say: **le seizième siècle**
or simply: **le XVIe**	Say: **le seizième.**

Roman numerals are quite often written as small capitals:

the seventeenth century = **le XVIe siècle** *or* **le XVIe**

For *in* use **au** (note that **siècle** is often omitted):

in the 17th century   = say: **au dix-septième siècle** *or* **au dix-septième**

early / late

début and **fin** are used rather than adjectives:

in the early 12th century	= **au début du douzième (siècle)**
in the late 14th century	= **à/vers la fin du quatorzième (siècle)**

Note the use of **du** in the following:

a 16th-century church	=	**une église du XVIᵉ siècle (*or* du seizième)**
19th-century novelists	=	**les romanciers du 19ᵉ siècle (*or* du dix-neuvième)**

See also *Days of the week, Months of the year*, and *Festivals*.

Time units

Here is a list of the main time divisions:

second	=	**seconde** *f*
minute	=	**minute** *f*
hour	=	**heure** *f*
day	=	**jour** *m* / **journée** *f*
week	=	**semaine** *f*
month	=	**mois** *m*
year	=	**an** *m* / **année** *f*
century	=	**siècle** *m*

French paired forms (*an / année; jour / journée etc.*)

General guidelines:

Use the masculine forms:

● when precise periods of time are referred to:

for two years	=	**pendant deux ans**
three days running	=	**trois jours de suite**

● in greetings (**bonjour, bonsoir**)

● in frequency expressions:

twice a day	=	**deux fois par jour**
once a year	=	**une fois par an**

Use the feminine forms:

● in wishes:

| Happy New Year | = **Bonne année** |
| Have a nice day/evening | = **Bonne journée/soirée** |

● when the nature or content of the period is specified (even with numbers):

his two years in government	= **ses deux années de gouvernement**
throughout the Cold War years	= **pendant toutes les années de guerre froide**
all the (wine harvest) years are good	= **toutes les années (de vendange) sont bonnes**

● when an adjective or other expression qualifying the time expression is present:

a wonderful evening	= **une excellente soirée**
a year of study	= **une année d'études**
a morning of bitter fighting	= **une matinée de combats acharnés**
all the previous years	= **toutes les années précédentes**

But there are cases where the use of masculine or feminine forms varies from word to word:

le premier/dernier jour *but* **la première/dernière année**

deux jours de suite *but* **deux années de suite**

jour après jour *but* **année après année**

d'un jour à l'autre *but* **d'une année à l'autre**

les deux jours à venir *but* **les deux années à venir**

half

When **demi** precedes the noun (normally with hyphen) it does not agree:

| half an hour | = **une demi-heure** |
| a half day | = **une demi-journée** |

When it follows it agrees:

an hour and a half	=	**une heure et demie**

Duration
Time taken
Note the following constructions:

il (me/lui, etc.) faut + (time expression) + **pour faire quelque chose**
qch met + (time expression) + **pour faire quelque chose**
cela (me/lui, etc.) prend + (time expression)
je prends/cela (me/lui, etc.) prend + (time expression)

how long does it take?	=	**combien de temps faut-il?**
it took me a week	=	**cela m'a pris une semaine** or **il m'a fallu une semaine**
I only took an hour to finish it	=	**je n'ai mis qu'une heure pour le terminer**
the letter took a full month to arrive	=	**la lettre a mis un mois entier pour arriver**
it'll take at least a year	=	**il faudra une bonne année** or **il faudra au moins un an**
the train takes more than two hours	=	**le train met plus de deux heures**
it should take you less than a week	=	**cela devrait vous prendre moins d'une semaine**

Also:

it'll only take a moment	=	**c'est l'affaire de quelques instants** or **cela ne demandera qu'une minute**

Expressions with prepositions
Translating *in*
en says how long something takes/took/will take; **dans** says in how long from now something will take place:

we'll finish it in an hour

- = **nous le terminerons en une heure** (= *1 hour's work*)
- = **nous le terminerons dans une heure** (= *end of work 1 hour from now*)

the rate will go down two per cent in less than six weeks

- = **la cote va baisser de deux pour cent en moins de six semaines** (= *the process will take less than six weeks*)
- = **la cote va baisser de deux pour cent dans moins de six semaines** (= *it will be reduced in one go at a moment less than 6 weeks hence*)

Other examples:

she's expecting her third child in five weeks	= **elle attend son troisième enfant dans cinq semaines**
she's expecting her third child in five years	= **elle attend son troisième enfant en cinq ans**
that'll be the third time they've voted in less than a year	= **cela fera la troisième fois qu'ils votent en moins d'un an**
it's taking place in two weeks	= **cela aura lieu dans deux semaines**
we can expect a replacement in a month	= **nous pouvons nous attendre à avoir une remplaçante dans un mois**
the next exhibition will be in ten years' time	= **la prochaine exposition est prévue pour dans dix ans**
it'll be over in no time	= **ce sera terminé en un rien de temps**

how long and expressions translating *for*

Use **pendant** to translate *for* when speaking of how long something took/takes. Most cases refer to the past and use the Perfect (passé composé) tense:

I worked there for ten years	= **j'ai travaillé là pendant dix ans**
Chirac directed foreign policy for two years	= **Chirac a conduit la politique étrangère pendant deux ans**
she collaborated on it for five months	= **elle y a collaboré pendant cinq mois**

Use **depuis** for cases where the action started in the past and is still going on (Present tense in French) or was still going on (Imperfect tense in French):

the rate has been increasing considerably for three years	= **le taux est en forte augmentation depuis trois ans**
the refugees have been dreaming of a safe haven for at least eighteen months	= **les réfugiés rêvent d'un havre de sécurité depuis au moins dix-huit mois**
they had been researching it for ten months	= **ils menaient une enquête là-dessus depuis dix mois**
that had been the case for going on ten years	= **c'était le cas depuis bientôt dix ans**
they've been engaged for some time now	= **ils sont fiancés depuis déjà quelque temps**

The tense becomes Perfect (passé composé) or Pluperfect when results, or a series of separate actions or events, are referred to:

for four years we have done deals with various companies	= **depuis quatre ans nous avons conclu des affaires avec diverses compagnies**

Use **pour** for time still to come, e.g. when speaking of intentions, plans, etc.:

he has signed with the team for four years	= **il a signé avec le club pour quatre ans**
no, I'm only here for five days	= **non, je ne suis là que pour cinq jours**
they've frozen all promotions for a year	= **ils ont gelé toutes les promotions pour un an**

With verbs such as **attendre, rester,** *for* may not need to be translated at all:

she'll have to wait for at least three months	= **elle devra attendre au moins trois mois**

they stayed for a week = **ils sont restés une semaine**

over

Note the use of **au cours de**:

rates will rise over the coming months	= **les taux vont augmenter au cours des mois à venir**
they've met several times over the past few weeks	= **ils se sont rencontrés plusieurs fois au cours des dernières semaines**
pollution has gone up over the past few weeks	= **la pollution a augmenté au cours des dernières semaines**

Note the use of **de** in expressions like *two-minute delay*:

a two-month suspension	= **une suspension de deux mois**
a ten-year drought	= **une sécheresse de dix ans**
a six-month sentence	= **une peine de six mois**

Time when

In the past

Note the use of expressions like **il y a/cela fait/voici maintenant** e.g. when translating English *ago/it's been*, etc.:

he became the number one player a year ago	= **il est devenu joueur numéro un il y a un an**
the rate was two per cent three years ago	= **le taux était de deux pour cent il y a trois ans**
it's been ten years since she died	= **cela fait dix ans qu'elle est morte**
he was taken to hospital a month ago now	= **voici maintenant un mois qu'il a été hospitalisé**

AFTER/LATER/NEXT/LAST

the year after	= **l'année d'après** *(Note: the* **d'** *is obligatory)*
after three hours	= **au bout de trois heures**
the next month	= **le mois suivant**
last year	= **l'année dernière**

the month before last = **il y a deux mois**

In the future

we are expecting the = **on attend l'inspecteur d'un jour à**
inspector any day now   **l'autre**

we'll know this coming = **on le saura la semaine qui vient**
week   *(colloquial) or* **au cours de la**
    semaine à venir

a month from tomorrow = **dans un mois demain**

For phrases with *in* see the section on expressions with
prepositions (see above, p. 18).

Frequency
How often

When translating *every*, expressions with **tous/toutes** are
preferable to those with **chaque**:

how often do you get the = **vous recevez la revue tous les**
magazine?   **combien?** *(colloquial)*

every Thursday/week = **tous les jeudis/toutes les semaines**
    or **chaque jeudi/semaine**

When translating ordinal numbers after *every*, use
cardinal numbers in French:

every second Tuesday/ = **tous les deux mardis/mois**
month

How much an/per hour

Use **à** when referring to the time units which indicate
frequency:

paid by the month = **payé au mois**
rented by the week = **loué à la semaine**

Use **par** for money (etc.) rates per period:

how much do you get = **combien gagnez-vous par semaine?**
a/per week?

2,000 pounds a month   =   **deux mille livres par mois**

Progression: *jour après jour, d'un jour à l'autre, de jour en jour*

Expressions with **après** usually refer to repeated activities; this sometimes has overtones of drudgery, tedium, etc.

this consists of slanting the bottles day after day/every single day	=	**cela consiste à incliner les bouteilles jour après jour**
the crowd gathers round the palace day after day/every single day	=	**la foule se rassemble jour après jour autour du palais**
he tried day in day out to win her approval	=	**il s'efforçait jour après jour de gagner son approbation**
she is watching their daily life month in month out	=	**elle observe mois après mois leur vie quotidienne**
month in month out/ every single month, they systematically buy up shares on the Stock Exchange	=	**ils font des rachats successifs en Bourse mois après mois**

D'un jour (etc.) à l'autre has two meanings:
- any X now

it could happen at any moment	=	**cela peut arriver d'un moment à l'autre**
I'm expecting to be called up any day now	=	**je m'attends à être mobilisé d'un jour à l'autre**

- X by X; from one X to the next (*usually accompanied by* **plus/moins** *or by verbs indicating a progression or tendency*)

this is growing month by month	=	**cela s'accroît d'un mois à l'autre**

a tendency becoming more marked day by day	=	**une tendance d'un jour à l'autre plus marquée**
she's improving her Spanish week by week	=	**elle se perfectionne en espagnol d'une semaine à l'autre**
this varies little from one year to the next	=	**cela varie peu d'une année à l'autre**

● each and every (*less common*)

| each and every year/ every year without fail, the US universities produce Nobel Prize winners | = | **d'année en année** *or* **année après année, les universités des USA produisent des prix Nobel** |

De jour en jour, etc. can also be used to mean *X by X*:

| getting smaller day by day | = | **plus petit de jour en jour** |
| the choir improves year by year | = | **la chorale se perfectionne d'année en année** |

For **jour/journée** vs. **an/année** see *Time units*.

....

The clock

Here is a list of key times. As in English, French distinguishes between colloquial usage and a more official one (often based on written sources such as timetables):

| one-ten *or* ten minutes past one | = | **une heure dix** |
| 1.10 p.m. | = | **13 h 10** (*say*: **treize heures dix**) |

Note that French never omits the word **heures**.

Colloquial, everyday usage

| it is four o'clock *or* it's four | = | **il est quatre heures** |

Note the use of **de** + definite article to translate *in* in the following:

it was three o'clock in the morning	=	**il était trois heures du matin**
it was three o'clock in the afternoon	=	**il était trois heures de l'après-midi**
it was eight o'clock in the evening	=	**il était huit heures du soir**

French, like English, distinguishes between minutes up to thirty, viewed as being after the hour, and minutes from 31, seen as being before the next hour:

two minutes past four	=	**quatre heures deux**
ten past three *or* three-ten	=	**trois heures dix**
twenty-five minutes past two *or* two twenty-five	=	**deux heures vingt-cinq**
eighteen minutes past ten *or* ten eighteen	=	**dix heures dix-huit**
a quarter past six	=	**six heures et quart**
half past seven	=	**sept heures et demie** (*see above for rules on the agreement of* demi)
twenty-eight minutes to two	=	**deux heures moins vingt-huit**
twenty to three	=	**trois heures moins vingt**
five to ten	=	**dix heures moins cinq**
a quarter to three	=	**trois heures moins le quart**
a quarter to midday	=	**midi moins le quart**
half past midnight	=	**minuit et demi**

Official (using the twenty-four hour clock)

4.00 *or* 0400 hours	= **quatre heures**	(*write* 4 h 00)
4.02	= **quatre heures deux**	(*write* 4 h 02)
4.15	= **quatre heures quinze**	(*write* 4 h 15)
4.30	= **quatre heures trente**	(*write* 4 h 30)

5.37	= **cinq heures trente-sept**	(*write* 5 h 37)
6.55	= **six heures cinquante-cinq**	(*write* 6 h 55)
12.00	= **douze heures**	(*write* 12 h 00)
16.00 *or* 4 pm	= **seize heures**	(*write* 16 h 00)
20.30 *or* 8.30 pm	= **vingt heures trente**	(*write* 20 h 30)
24.00 *or* 12 midnight	= **vingt-quatre heures**	(*write* 24 h 00)

You will quite often hear French speakers, especially on the radio, using forms like **il est onze heures (et) quatre minutes**. The foreign learner does not need to use these very full forms (mainly used for minutes up to 9 after the hour) except when requiring extra special clarity.

Asking the time

what time is it *or* what's the time?	= **quelle heure est-il?** *or (more colloquial)* **il est quelle heure?**
could you tell me the time?	= **pouvez-vous me donner l'heure?**
do you have the time?	= **vous avez l'heure?** (*colloquial*)

Talking about the time

Exact or approximate time

juste and **environ** do not agree. Adjectives such as **précis** or **passé** agree with **heures**.

EXACT

it's exactly three	= **il est trois heures précises**
on the stroke of four	= **à quatre heures juste/précises**
on the dot of five	= **à cinq heures précises**

APPROXIMATE

see you about two	= **rendez-vous vers deux heures**
it arrived just before seven	= **c'est arrivé peu avant sept heures**
they left just after ten	= **elles sont parties peu après dix heures**

it's gone nine = **il est neuf heures passées**

it's just gone three = **il est à peine trois heures**

Various time expressions with prepositions

BY, FOR, AND UNTIL

it must be ready by ten = **il faut que ce soit prêt avant dix heures** *or* **à dix heures au plus tard**

Note that *until* is **jusqu'à** but *not until* is **pas avant**:

wait until five = **attendez jusqu'à cinq heures** *or* *(colloquial)* **attendez cinq heures**

I won't be here till seven = **je ne serai pas là avant sept heures**

For is translated as **pour** here, as future time and plans are involved:

have it ready for *or* by six = **préparez-le pour six heures**

And, with a different sense of *by*:

it's 5 by my watch = **il est cinq heures à ma montre**

FROM AND TO

de and **à** are often sufficient; for extra clarity use **à partir de** and **jusqu'à**:

open from ten to twelve = **ouvert de dix à douze heures**

she's available from nine = **elle est disponible à partir de neuf heures**

they work on to ten = **ils travaillent jusqu'à dix heures**

Place

Nationalities and languages

Nationalities

Use of capital/lower-case letters

Use capitals for nouns referring to people of specific nationalities:

a Scot	=	**un Écossais**
an Englishwoman	=	**une Anglaise**
several Frenchmen	=	**plusieurs Français**
that Dane	=	**ce Danois**
the Italians	=	**les Italiens**
a Chinese woman	=	**une Chinoise**

Use lower-case letters for adjectives (see also *Languages*, below)

the French state	=	**l'État français**
Turkish trains	=	**les trains turcs**
Japanese customs	=	**les coutumes japonaises**

Words for nationalities

Where English often has one word for a nationality and another for the adjective (*Dane/Danish; Frenchman/French*), French usually uses the same form as adjective (lower case) and as noun referring to a person or people (capitals):

Danish	=	**danois/danoise**
a Dane	=	**un Danois/une Danoise**
the Danes	=	**les Danois**

But note that *Finnish* has two translations:

a Finn	=	**un Finlandais/une Finlandaise**

to speak Finnish   = **parler le finnois**

Use of *ce* and *il / elle* as subject of verb *être*

Use **il/elle** when the verb is followed by an adjective (lower-case initial letter).

Use **ce** with article (**un/une/des**) + noun (capital initial letter).

he is French   = **il est français**

he is a Frenchman   = **c'est un Français**

she is Scottish   = **elle est écossaise**

she is a Scot   = **c'est une Écossaise**

This also works for regions (see below):

they are Bavarian   = **ils sont bavarois**

they are Bavarians   = **ce sont des Bavarois**

Note the following, however, where a number is present:

there are 1.3 million of = **ils sont 1,3 millions de Français**
  them who have   **par acquisition nés hors de France**
  acquired French
  nationality but were
  born outside France

When the subject is a noun (including proper nouns), use the adjective form (lower case):

Lars is Danish *or* Lars = **Lars est danois**
  is a Dane

his wife is Turkish   = **sa femme est turque**

Never use **un/une** + noun in such examples.

The forms with **un/une** (with **ce** as subject) must however be used when there is a complement (e.g. an adjective or a relative clause):

he's a young Greek   = **c'est un jeune Grec**

she's an Egyptian from   = **c'est une Égyptienne du Caire**
  Cairo

See also *Shops, trades, jobs, and professions* and *Artists and their works.*

Talking about people's origins

Besides saying **elle est danoise/c'est une Danoise**, note the following:

she comes from Italy	= **elle vient d'Italie**
she was born in Algeria	= **elle est née en Algérie**
he's a Spanish national	= **c'est un ressortissant espagnol**
they are of Belgian extraction	= **elles sont d'origine belge**
they are Belgians by birth	= **elles sont Belges d'origine**
he is a Norwegian citizen	= **il est citoyen norvégien**

Note that, as often in English, there are compound forms in French, the first element of which normally ends in **-o**:

Italian-American immigrants	= **des immigrés italo-américains**

Languages

The names of languages are masculine and use the definite article. Write them with a lower-case initial letter:

English is fascinating	= **l'anglais est passionnant**
German is widely spoken	= **l'allemand se parle partout**
to learn Chinese	= **apprendre le chinois**

But use no article after **en**:

say it in Russian	= **dis-le en russe**
a book in Japanese	= **un livre en japonais**

| to translate something into Spanish | = **traduire quelque chose en espagnol** |

The article is also optional after **parler**:

she speaks German	= **elle parle allemand** or **l'allemand**
I speak Arabic	= **je parle arabe** or **l'arabe**
their child is starting to speak Portuguese	= **leur enfant commence à parler portugais** or **le portugais**

The **le** is more likely when **parler** is qualified by an adverb:

| they speak Russian fluently | = **elles parlent couramment le russe** |

Translating adjectives

In many cases, both languages use an adjective:

the Russian language	= **la langue russe**
a Chinese word	= **un mot chinois**
a Swedish proverb	= **un proverbe suédois**
an English term	= **un terme anglais**

But when you mean *relating to* or *about* the language use **de**:

my German teacher	= **mon professeur d'allemand**
her Japanese class	= **son cours de japonais**
a new Turkish course	= **une nouvelle méthode de turc**
a Swedish dictionary	= **un dictionnaire de suédois**

However, for bilingual dictionaries adjective forms are used:

| a new German-English dictionary | = **un nouveau dictionnaire allemand-anglais** |

When you need to make it clear that something is *in* the language, **en** is best:

| a Spanish broadcast | = **une émission en espagnol** |

Contrast:

| a French book | = **un livre français** (*published in France, not necessarily in French*) |
| | = **un livre en français** (*in the French language, wherever published*) |

There are a few special words for forms ending in
-*speaker*/-*speaking*. Here is a list:

an English-speaker	= **un** *or* **une anglophone**
a French-speaking guide	= **un guide francophone**
Spanish-speaking	= **hispanophone**
German-speaking	= **germanophone**
Portuguese-speaking	= **lusophone**
Arabic-speaking	= **arabophone**
Russian-speaking	= **russophone**

See also *Countries and continents*.

....

Countries and continents

Continents

Note that the names of continents are all feminine and
should be written with a capital letter, usually preceded
by the definite article, except after **en**:

Africa	= **l'Afrique** *f*
America	= **l'Amérique** *f*
Asia	= **l'Asie** *f*
Europe	= **l'Europe** *f*

Similarly, terms for other major areas of the world:

| Oceania | = **l'Océanie** *f* |
| Polynesia | = **la Polynésie** |

| Siberia | = **la Sibérie** |

But the following two terms are masculine:

| the Arctic | = **l'Arctique** *m* |
| the Antarctic | = **l'Antarctique** *m* |

Terms for sub-divisions also require the definite article:

Asia minor	= **l'Asie mineure**
Central America	= **l'Amérique centrale**
Equatorial Africa	= **l'Afrique équatoriale**

And the same is true of expressions using other adjectives:

| deepest Africa | = **l'Afrique profonde** |

Countries

See *Islands* for names of islands which are also countries, such as *Cuba, Cyprus*, etc.

Names of countries should be written with a capital letter and preceded by the definite article (except where indicated below).

While many country names, especially European ones, are feminine singular, there are a number of masculine ones.

Common feminine names include:

China	= **la Chine**
Egypt	= **l'Égypte**
England	= **l'Angleterre**
France	= **la France**
Greece	= **la Grèce**
India	= **l'Inde**
Ireland	= **l'Irlande**
Italy	= **l'Italie**

Russia	=	**la Russie**
Scotland	=	**l'Écosse**
Spain	=	**l'Espagne**
Switzerland	=	**la Suisse**

Here is a list of masculine country names:

Afghanistan	=	**l'Afghanistan** (*all other* **-stans** *are also masculine*)
Angola	=	**l'Angola**
Bangladesh	=	**le Bangladesh**
Benin	=	**le Bénin**
Brazil	=	**le Brésil**
Burkina Faso	=	**le Burkina Faso**
Burundi	=	**le Burundi**
Cambodia	=	**le Cambodge**
Cameroon	=	**le Cameroun**
Canada	=	**le Canada**
Chad	=	**le Tchad**
Chile	=	**le Chili**
the Congo	=	**le Congo**
Costa Rica	=	**le Costa Rica**
Denmark	=	**le Danemark**
Ecuador	=	**l'Équateur**
Gabon	=	**le Gabon**
Ghana	=	**le Ghana**
Guatemala	=	**le Guatemala**
Honduras	=	**le Honduras**
Iran	=	**l'Iran**
Iraq	=	**l'Irak**
Japan	=	**le Japon**
Kenya	=	**le Kenya**
Kuweit	=	**le Koweït**
Laos	=	**le Laos**

Lebanon	=	**le Liban**
Lesotho	=	**le Lesotho**
Liberia	=	**le Libéria**
Liechtenstein	=	**le Liechtenstein**
Luxemburg	=	**le Luxembourg**
Malawi	=	**le Malawi**
Mali	=	**le Mali**
Mexico	=	**le Mexique**
Morocco	=	**le Maroc**
Mozambique	=	**le Mozambique**
Nepal	=	**le Népal**
Nicaragua	=	**le Nicaragua**
Niger	=	**le Niger**
Nigeria	=	**le Nigeria**
Pakistan	=	**le Pakistan**
Panama	=	**le Panama**
Paraguay	=	**le Paraguay**
Peru	=	**le Pérou**
Portugal	=	**le Portugal**
Rwanda	=	**le Rwanda**
El Salvador	=	**le Salvador**
Senegal	=	**le Sénégal**
Sri Lanka	=	**le Sri Lanka**
the Sudan	=	**le Soudan**
Surinam	=	**le Surinam**
Swaziland	=	**le Swaziland**
Togo	=	**le Togo**
Uganda	=	**l'Ouganda**
Uruguay	=	**l'Uruguay**
the Vatican	=	**le Vatican**
Venezuela	=	**le Venezuela**
Vietnam	=	**le Viêt Nam** *or* **le Vietnam**

the Yemen	= **le Yémen**
Zaire	= **le Zaïre**
Zimbabwe	= **le Zimbabwe**

Note also:

| Wales | = **le Pays de Galles** |

Countries with plural names:

the Netherlands	= **les Pays-Bas** *mpl*
the Philippines	= **les Philippines** *fpl*
the United States	= **les États-Unis** *mpl*

See also *Islands* for groups of islands such as *the Orkneys*.

The following examples show the use of the definite article:

Scotland is a mountainous country	= **l'Écosse est un pays montagneux**
they like Japan	= **ils aiment le Japon**
we know Greece quite well	= **nous connaissons assez bien la Grèce**
to fly to the Philippines	= **s'envoler pour les Philippines**

Country names including *North* etc. also require the definite article:

| East Germany | = **l'Allemagne de l'Est** |
| South Yemen | = **le Yémen du Sud** |

But **Israël** is not preceded by an article:

| to visit Israel | = **visiter Israël** |
| peace beween Israel and Jordan | = **la paix entre Israël et la Jordanie** |

Translating *to* **and** *in*

English contrasts *to* for movement with *in* for position:

to go *to* France/to be *in* France; to travel *to* Germany/to stay *in* Germany; to fly *to* Japan/to work *in* Japan, etc.

but:

French uses the same word for *to* and *in* but varies between **en** and **au/aux** according to the name of the country. There is no definite article after **en**.

The rules are as follows:

● Use **en** with feminine names of countries and continents:

to go to France	= **aller en France**
to live in Finland	= **vivre en Finlande**
to live in North Korea	= **vivre en Corée du Nord**
to go to south-East Asia	= **aller en Asie du sud-est**

● Use **en** with masculine names of countries beginning with a vowel (or mute h):

to go to Afghanistan	= **aller en Afghanistan**
to live in Ecuador	= **vivre en Équateur**

● Use **au** with masculine names of countries beginning with a consonant (or aspirate h):

to go to Japan	= **aller au Japon**
to go to Wales	= **aller au Pays de Galles**
to live in Japan	= **vivre au Japon**
to live in Honduras	= **vivre au Honduras**

● Use **aux** with plural names of countries (of either gender):

to go to the United States/the Philippines	= **aller aux États-Unis/aux Philippines**
to live in the United States/the Philippines	= **vivre aux États-Unis/aux Philippines**

Translating adjectives: *français* or *de France* or *de la France*?

There are no fixed rules here, but the following examples should be of some help:

● The first group use an adjective:

French cooking	= **la cuisine française**
the French Revolution	= **la révolution française**
the Egyptian army	= **l'armée égyptienne**
the German government	= **le gouvernement allemand**
the Italian nation	= **la nation italienne**
Russian traditions	= **les traditions russes**
African/Chinese literature	= **la littérature africaine/chinoise**
a Pakistani town	= **une ville pakistanaise**
Brazilian elections	= **les élections brésiliennes**

● **de** or **du** are used for most place names:

the Gulf of Finland	= **le golfe de Finlande**
the Mozambique channel	= **le canal du Mozambique**
the Gulf of Guinea	= **le golfe de Guinée**

but:

the Persian Gulf	= **le golfe Persique**

● For some combinations, French prefers **de** alone for feminine countries and **du** for masculine ones:

the history of France/of Gabon	= **l'histoire de France/du Gabon**
the king of Norway/of Lesotho	= **le roi de Norvège/du Lesotho**
the French/Zimbabwean team	= **l'équipe de France/du Zimbabwe**
the Greek/Swaziland embassy	= **l'ambassade de Grèce/du Swaziland**
the French/Japanese ambassador	= **l'ambassadeur de France/du Japon**

but note:

the French capital *or* the
capital of France = **la capitale de la France**

Where country and continent names are used like adjectives (but not in adjective form, i.e. *Asia* not *Asian*), the normal pattern is to use **de** + definite article:

the Asia question = **la question de l'Asie**

the Europe vote = **le vote de l'Europe**

the Angola dossier = **le dossier de l'Angola**

Note also:

the China trade = **le commerce avec la Chine**

the Syria-Iraq border = **la frontière irako-syrienne** *or* **entre l'Irak et la Syrie**

See also *Islands* and *Points of the compass*.

Regions, including: French provinces and regions; French departments; British regions and counties; US States; Swiss cantons

Names

French provinces

Prior to the French Revolution, France was divided into provinces. Although abolished at that time, their names are still used today, and some have reappeared in the modern *Régions (see below)*.

The names of most provinces are feminine and are preceded by the definite article (as with countries).

Where there is an adjective form derived from the name of the province, this adjective may also designate the inhabitants, in which case it is written with a capital

letter. See also below under *Modern French regions* if the
name appears again there:

Feminine names:

Alsace	= l'Alsace
Aquitaine	= l'Aquitaine
the Auvergne	= l'Auvergne
Brittany	= la Bretagne
Burgundy	= la Bourgogne
Champagne	= la Champagne (champenois; un Champenois/une Champenoise)
the Ile de France	= l'Île de France
Lorraine	= la Lorraine
Normandy	= la Normandie (normand; un Normand/une Normande)
Picardy	= la Picardie
Provence	= la Provence (provençal; un Provençal/une Provençale)
Savoy	= la Savoie (savoyard; un Savoyard/une Savoyarde)
Touraine	= la Touraine (tourangeau; un Tourangeau/une Tourangelle)

Masculine names:

the Béarn	= le Béarn (béarnais; un Béarnais/une Béarnaise)
the Berry	= le Berry (berrichon; un Berrichon/une Berrichonne)
the Languedoc	= le Languedoc (languedocien; un Languedocien/une Languedocienne)
the Limousin	= le Limousin
Maine	= le Maine
Poitou	= le Poitou (poitevin; un Poitevin/une Poitevine)
Roussillon	= le Roussillon

Modern French regions

The names for most modern regions have corresponding adjectives. Note the exceptions where **habitant de** is used:

l'Alsace *f* (alsacien; un Alsacien/une Alsacienne)

l'Aquitaine *f* (un habitant de l'Aquitaine *or* de la région Aquitaine)

l'Auvergne *f* (auvergnat; un Auvergnat/une Auvergnate)

la Basse-Normandie (bas-normand; un habitant de la Basse-Normandie)

la Bourgogne (bourguignon; un Bourguignon/une Bourguignonne)

la Bretagne (breton; un Breton/une Bretonne)

le Centre (un habitant du Centre *or* de la région (du) Centre)

Champagne-Ardenne (un habitant de Champagne-Ardenne *or* de la région Champagne-Ardenne)

la Franche-Comté (franc-comtois; un Franc-comtois/une Franc-comtoise)

la Haute-Normandie (haut-normand; un habitant de la Haute-Normandie)

l'Île-de-France *f* (francilien; un Francilien/une Francilienne)

Languedoc-Roussillon (un habitant de Languedoc-Roussillon *or* de la région Languedoc-Roussillon)

le Limousin (limousin; un Limousin/une Limousine)

la Lorraine (lorrain; un Lorrain/une Lorraine)

Midi-Pyrénées (un habitant de Midi-Pyrénées *or* de la région Midi-Pyrénées)

Nord-Pas-de-Calais (un habitant de Nord-Pas-de-Calais *or* de la région Nord-Pas-de-Calais)

les Pays de la Loire *mpl* (un habitant des Pays de la Loire *or* un habitant de la région des Pays de la Loire)

la Picardie (picard; un Picard/une Picarde)

Poitou-Charentes (un habitant de Poitou-Charentes *or* de la région Poitou-Charentes)

Provence-Alpes-Côte d'Azur (un habitant de Provence-Alpes-Côte d'Azur *or* de la région Provence-Alpes-Côte d'Azur)

Rhône-Alpes (rhône-alpin; un habitant de Rhône-Alpes *or* de la région Rhône-Alpes)

From the above we can see that French has more nouns
for the inhabitants than English has:

the Bretons   = **les Bretons**

the people of Languedoc = **les Languedociens**

French departments

French department names are of several types and the
syntax of sentences including them is varied. They
include:

- simple names: **le Loiret; la Lozère; les Yvelines**
- compound hyphenated names:
- with preceding modifier: **le Bas-Rhin; la Haute-Loire**
- with following modifier: **la Charente-Maritime; les
  Pyrénées-Orientales**
- compound names with *de*: **la Côte-d'Or; les Côtes-
  d'Armor; le Pas-de-Calais**
- compound names with *et*: **l'Ille-et-Vilaine; la Meurthe-et-
  Moselle**

As can be seen from the above examples, names can be
singular or plural.

Canadian provinces

British Columbia	=	**la Colombie britannique**
New Brunswick	=	**le Nouveau-Brunswick**
Newfoundland	=	**Terre-Neuve** (*note no article*)
North-West Territories	=	**les Territoires du Nord-Ouest**
Nova Scotia	=	**la Nouvelle-Écosse**
Prince Edward Island	=	**l'île du Prince-Édouard**
Quebec	=	**le Québec**

Other provinces keep their English spelling and are
masculine: **l'Alberta; le Manitoba; l'Ontario; le
Saskatchewan; le Yukon.**

Belgian provinces

Brabant	= **le Brabant**
East Flanders	= **la Flandre orientale**
Hainault	= **le Hainault**
Limburg	= **le Limbourg**
Luxemburg	= **le Luxembourg** *or* **la province du Luxembourg**
West Flanders	= **la Flandre occidentale**

The other provinces bear the names of cities: **la province de Liège, de Namur, d'Anvers** (= *Antwerp*).

Swiss cantons

the Valais	= **le Valais**

Several cantons bear the name of the chief town (in its French version where appropriate). In such cases one needs to say **le canton de** +:

Genève, Lucerne, Berne, Neuchâtel, Fribourg

St Gall (German *St Gallen*), **Schaffhouse** (German *Schaffhausen*), **Soleure** (German *Solothurn*)

One also uses the full form for **le canton de Vaud**. This is the only possible form, maybe to avoid confusion with **veau** (= *veal/calf*).

Some German-speaking Swiss cantons keep their German name in French; they are all masculine:

l'Uri; le Schwyz; le Glarus; l'Appenzell; le Zug

Other cantons have separate French forms:

Aargau	= **l'Argovie** *f*
Graubünden	= **les Grisons** *mpl*
Thurgau	= **la Thurgovie**
Ticino	= **le Tessin**
Unterwalden	= **l'Unterwald** *m*

British regions and counties

French does not have separate names for these and they are all masculine, with the exception of:

Cornwall	= **la Cornouailles**

Otherwise:

Kent	= **le Kent**
Perthshire	= **le Perthshire**
Yorkshire	= **le Yorkshire**

etc.

US States

Many US States have the same form in French as in English. Here is a list of the main cases with a different form:

California	= **la Californie** (*names ending in -nie are feminine*)
Carolina	= **la Caroline** (*hence*: North/South Carolina = **la Caroline du Nord/du Sud**)
Florida	= **la Floride**
Hawaii	= **Hawaï** (*normally* m; *note no article*)
Louisiana	= **la Louisiane**
New Mexico	= **le Nouveau Mexique**
Virginia	= **la Virginie** (West Virginia = **la Virginie occidentale**)
Pennsylvania	= **la Pennsylvanie**

Note also (though it is not a state)

New England	= **la Nouvelle Angleterre**

But note that *New* remains in its English form in **le New Hampshire** and **le New Jersey**.

Apart from the cases listed above, most state names are
masculine, including those which might appear
feminine because they end in *a*:

l'Alaska *m*; **l'Arizona** *m*; **le Dakota (du Nord/du Sud);
l'Indiana** *m*; **le Montana; le Nebraska.**

Definite article

As can be seen from the above lists, French uses the
article with region names:

to visit Hainault	= **visiter le Hainault**
in deepest Berry	= **dans le Berry profond**
to like Ontario	= **aimer l'Ontario**
to visit (the) Cher	= **visiter le Cher**
they have visited Yorkshire	= **ils ont visité le Yorkshire**
we like Kent	= **nous aimons le Kent**
Arizona is beautiful	= **l'Arizona est beau**
I like California	= **j'aime la Californie**
I like Ticino	= **j'aime le Tessin**
the Valais is beautiful	= **le Valais est beau**
do you know Graubünden?	= **connaissez-vous les Grisons?**

Exceptions to the general use of the article are as follows:

to visit Newfoundland	= **visiter Terre-Neuve**
do you know Hawaii?	= **connaissez-vous Hawaï?**

Translating *of*

Normally use **de** + definite article.

Modern French *régions* use the definite article when
they are single words, but none when they are
complex (several words); in the latter case, the words **la
région** are often added; this is also the case for Swiss
cantons.

the problems of Alsace	= **les problèmes de l'Alsace**
the loss of Alsace and Corsica	= **la perte de l'Alsace et de la Corse**
the problems of Rhône-Alpes	= **les problèmes de la région Rhône-Alpes**
the problems of Midi-Pyrénées	= **les problèmes de la région Midi-Pyrénées**
a regional councillor of Alsace	= **un conseiller régional de l'Alsace** *or* **d'Alsace**

Likewise:

de Provence-Côte d'Azur *or* **de la région Provence-Côte d'Azur**

de Champagne-Ardenne *or* **de la région Champagne-Ardenne**

For other regions, **de** + definite article is normal:

the problems of (the) Ille-et-Vilaine	= **les problèmes de l'Ille-et-Vilaine**
the roads of (the) Haut-Rhin	= **les routes du Haut-Rhin**
the state of Texas	= **l'état du Texas**

For Swiss cantons, when saying **le canton**, add **de** alone for **Vaud** or if the name is that of a town; otherwise use **de** + definite article:

the canton of Berne/Neuchâtel	= **le canton de Berne/de Neuchâtel**
the Valais	= **le canton du Valais**
the canton of Graubünden	= **le canton des Grisons**

For US States both **de** and **de la** can be found with feminine names:

the coast of Louisiana	= **les côtes de Louisiane** *or* **de la Louisiane**
the south of Florida	= **le sud de la Floride**

Titles

For titles, simply use **de**:

the duke of Berry	= **le duc de Berry**
the duchess of Kent	= **la duchesse de Kent**
the earl of Surrey	= **le comte de Surrey**
the elector of Saxony	= **l'électeur de Saxe**

See also *Forms of address*.

Translating English compound expressions

Where English uses an adjective, French does so too:

a Norman house	= **une maison normande**
Breton wardrobes	= **des armoires bretonnes**
Provençal cuisine	= **la cuisine provençale**

Where English uses a compound expression, French may use an adjective:

an Alsace accent	= **l'accent alsacien**
the Normandy coast	= **la côte normande**
the Berry countryside	= **la campagne berrichonne**
Lorraine cuisine	= **la cuisine lorraine**

But a construction with **de** is also normal:

an Alsace village	= **un village d'Alsace**
the Alsace chess champion	= **le champion d'Alsace d'échecs**

In our corpus **du Languedoc** is preferred to **languedocien/ne** with **vignoble, viticulteurs, sélection, coteaux, champion, vin, région**.

With French departments, usage is somewhat uncertain, but the normal position is as follows:

Use **de** with complex feminine names.

Use **de** or **de la** with simple feminine names (there is some variation here).

Use **du** with masculine names.

Use **de l'** with names beginning with a vowel or semi-vowel.

Use **des** with plural names.

● *de* (sometimes *de la*)

Haute-Garonne industries	= **les industries de Haute-Garonne**
Loire-Atlantique fishermen	= **les pêcheurs de Loire-Atlantique**
Saône-et-Loire wines	= **les vins de Saône-et-Loire**
Seine-Maritime ports	= **les ports de** or **de la Seine-Maritime**
Seine-et-Marne farmers	= **des agriculteurs de la Seine-et-Marne**
Seine-et-Marne hotels	= **les hôtels de Seine-et-Marne**

● **Either *de* or *de la***

Savoy roads	= **les routes de** or **de la Savoie**
Mayenne rivers	= **les rivières de** or **de la Mayenne**
the Vendée population	= **la population de** or *(better)* **de la Vendée**
the Meuse hills	= **les côtes/coteaux de la Meuse**

Similarly with **Corrèze; Guyane; Manche; Moselle; Nièvre; Sarthe; Vienne,** etc.

● *du/de la*

Finistère fishing ports	= **les ports de pêche du Finistère**
Rhône motorways	= **les autoroutes du Rhône**
Val-d'Oise problems	= **les problèmes du Val-d'Oise**

Similarly with **Calvados; Jura; Maine-et-Loire; Nord; Pas-de-Calais; Val-de-Marne; Var.**

● *de l'*

Ain towns	= **les villes de l'Ain**
Yonne representatives	= **les représentants de l'Yonne**

Similarly with **Allier; Eure; Indre; Isère; Yonne.**

● *des* **(sometimes** *de***)**

Ardennes woods	= **les bois des Ardennes**
Hauts-de-Seine representatives	= **des élus des Hauts-de-Seine**

Similarly with **Alpes-Maritimes; Bouches-du-Rhône; Vosges; Yvelines.**

With British counties, it is usual to use **de** + definite article:

Fife cuisine	= **la cuisine du Fife**
a Somerset accent	= **l'accent du Somerset**
Yorkshire people	= **les habitants du Yorkshire**
Sussex towns	= **les villes du Sussex**

For US States, apart from a few distinct adjectives (e.g. **new-yorkais; texan; californien**), French uses expressions with **de**.

It is always safe to use **de** + definite article:

Illinois representatives	= **les représentants de l'Illinois**
the New Mexico desert	= **le désert du Nouveau Mexique**
she spoke with a Louisiana accent	= **elle parlait avec l'accent de la Louisiane**

But **de** alone can be used for feminine states if there are no other complements:

the Florida countryside	= **les paysages de Floride**

Some Swiss cantons have adjectival forms: **bernois, valaisan, vaudois, tessinois:**

Valais cattle	=	**le bétail valaisan**
a Vaud accent	=	**l'accent vaudois**

Otherwise use constructions with **du/des** + canton name
or **du canton de** + canton name:

Uri people	=	**les gens de l'Uri**
Glarus problems	=	**les problèmes du Glarus**
Neuchâtel railways	=	**les chemins de fer du canton de Neuchâtel**

Translating *in, to,* and *from*

in and *to*

For old provinces, use **en** with feminine names and
masculine ones beginning with a vowel:

in Alsace/Normandy/ Aquitaine/Artois	=	**en Alsace/en Normandie/en Aquitaine/en Artois**

Use **dans le** for masculine names beginning with a
consonant:

in the Berry/Roussillon/ Poitou	=	**dans le Berry/dans le Roussillon/dans le Poitou**

For modern *régions*, **en** is usually acceptable, though
région is often added for the newer names (i.e. those
which are not identical with those of the older provinces
or consist of several words):

to live in/to go to Aquitaine	=	**vivre en/aller en Aquitaine**
to live in/to go to Poitou-Charentes	=	**vivre/aller en Poitou-Charentes** *or* **dans la région Poitou-Charentes**
to live in/to go to the Rhône-Alpes region	=	**vivre/aller en Rhône-Alpes** *or* **dans la région Rhône-Alpes**

Note the difference between the single names for old
provinces and compound names for modern *régions*:

| in/to the Languedoc | = | **dans le Languedoc** |
| in/to Languedoc-Roussillon | = | **en Languedoc-Roussillon** |

For French departments, use **en** for feminine names beginning with a consonant:

| to go to the Vendée | = | **se rendre en Vendée** |
| to live in Seine-et-Marne | = | **vivre en Seine-et-Marne** |

Aspirate h counts as a consonant:

| to go to Haute-Corse | = | **aller en Haute-Corse** |
| to live in Haute-Marne | = | **vivre en Haute-Marne** |

There is some hesitation, however, and examples like the following occur:

| to go to Haute-Loire | = | **aller en** or **dans la Haute-Loire** |
| to live in Ille-et-Vilaine | = | **vivre en Ille-et-Vilaine** or **dans l'Ille-et-Vilaine** |

For all names beginning with a vowel or semi-vowel, irrespective of gender, use **dans** + definite article:

to go to the Yonne	=	**aller dans l'Yonne**
to live in the Oise	=	**vivre dans l'Oise**
to go to the Ain	=	**aller dans l'Ain**
to live in the Allier	=	**habiter dans l'Allier**
to go to the Yvelines	=	**aller dans les Yvelines**
to live in the Ardennes	=	**habiter dans les Ardennes**
to live in the Aisne	=	**habiter dans l'Aisne**

And likewise **dans l'Ardèche, dans l'Ariège, dans l'Eure, dans l'Isère, dans l'Oise, dans l'Orne.**

For masculine names beginning with a consonant, use **dans le** and for plural names use **dans les.**

| to go to (the) Calvados | = | **aller dans le Calvados** |
| to live in the Tarn | = | **habiter dans le Tarn** |

For British regions and counties, use **dans le**:

to live in Berkshire	= **habiter dans le Berkshire**
to go to Surrey	= **aller dans le Surrey**
to go to the Midlands	= **aller dans les Midlands**

but note:

| to live in/to go to Cornwall | = **vivre/aller en Cornouailles** |

For US States, the rules are the same as for countries, i.e. use **en** for feminine names and masculine names beginning with a vowel; use **au** for masculine names beginning with a consonant:

to work in Louisiana	= **travailler en Louisiane**
to go to Louisiana	= **aller en Louisiane**
to live in Alaska	= **vivre en Alaska**
to send goods to Alaska	= **expédier des marchandises en Alaska**
to seek one's fortune in Texas	= **chercher fortune au Texas**
to go to Texas	= **aller au Texas**

Occasionally **dans le** is used with masculine names. Our corpus includes both the following:

| El Paso, in Texas | = **El Paso, au Texas** |
| Fort Worth, in Texas | = **Fort Worth, dans le Texas** |

but:

| in/to Hawaii | = **à Hawaï** |

For Swiss cantons, use **dans le/les** or **dans le canton de/du/des** (*which is always safe*):

| to live in the Valais | = **vivre dans le Valais** *or* **dans le canton du Valais** |
| to go to the Valais | = **aller dans le Valais** *or* **dans le canton du Valais** |

to live in Graubünden	= **vivre dans les Grisons**
to go to Ticino	= **aller dans le Tessin**
to live in the canton of Vaud	= **vivre dans le canton de Vaud**

Translating *from*

For French regions and provinces:

he comes from Alsace	= **il vient d'Alsace**
from the Ardennes to Alsace	= **des Ardennes à l'Alsace**
coming from the Berry	= **venu(e) du Berry**

but:

| elected members of/ from Normandy | = **des élus normands** |

Compare traditional provinces with modern regions:

| from the Languedoc | = **du Languedoc** |
| from Languedoc-Roussillon | = **de la région Languedoc-Roussillon** |

For French departments, the main hesitation concerns feminine singular names beginning with a consonant. Examples can be found both with **de** and with **de la**:

to come from Savoie	= **venir de Savoie** *or* **de la Savoie**
to come from the Dordogne	= **venir de Dordogne** *or* **de la Dordogne**
to come from the Meuse	= **venir de la Meuse**
to come from the Sarthe	= **venir de la Sarthe**

With words beginning with a vowel or semi-vowel use **de l'**:

| to come from the Oise/ the Yonne | = **venir de l'Oise/de l'Yonne** |

Compound names tend to have **de** if feminine and **du** if masculine:

to come from Seine-et-Marne	= **venir de Seine-et-Marne** *or* **de la Seine-et-Marne**
to come from Haute-Corse	= **venir de Haute-Corse**
to come from Loire-Atlantique	= **venir de Loire-Atlantique** *or* **de la Loire-Atlantique**
to come from the Val-d'Oise	= **venir du Val-d'Oise**

With simple masculine names use **du**:

to come from the Var	= **venir du Var**
to come from the Cher	= **venir du Cher**

With plural names use **des**:

to come from the Yvelines	= **venir des Yvelines**
to come from the Alpes-Maritimes	= **venir des Alpes-Maritimes**
to come from the Hauts-de-Seine	= **venir des Hauts-de-Seine**
to come from the Landes	= **venir des Landes**

For English counties and regions use **de** + definite article:

to come from Sussex/Yorkshire	= **venir du Sussex/du Yorkshire**
to come from the Midlands	= **venir des Midlands**
to come from Cornwall	= **venir de la Cornouailles**

For US States, use **de** for feminine names and for masculine ones beginning with a vowel; otherwise use **du**:

to come from Virginia	= **venir de Virginie**
to come from Illinois	= **venir d'Illinois** *or* **de l'Illinois**
to come from Montana	= **venir du Montana**

but:

| from Hawaii | = **d'Hawaï** |

For Swiss cantons use **du/des/de l'** or **du canton de** (*always safe*):

to come from the Valais	= **venir du Valais** *or* **du canton du Valais**
to come from the Vaud	= **venir du canton de Vaud**
to come from Ticino	= **venir du Tessin**

Islands

French island names fall into three main categories:

(a) The largest category consists of those which normally require the definite article. They are mostly feminine:

we like Sardinia	= **nous aimons la Sardaigne**
Sicily is beautiful	= **la Sicile est belle**
the climate of Martinique	= **le climat de la Martinique**

And also plural names:

| we know Fiji | = **nous connaissons les Fidji** *fpl* |

We can also include here the very large islands:

| Greenland | = **le Groënland** |
| Australia | = **l'Australie** *f* |

(b) Those in the second category (some of which are also independent countries) do not usually require the definite article.

| Bali | = **Bali** *m* |
| Ceylon | = **Ceylan** *m* |

Cuba	=	**Cuba** *m*
Cyprus	=	**Chypre** *f*
Formosa	=	**Formose** *m*
Haiti	=	**Haïti** *m*
Java	=	**Java** *m*
Malta	=	**Malte** *f*
Samoa	=	**Samoa** *m* (*but* Western Samoa = **les Samoa occidentales** *fpl*)
Taiwan	=	**Taiwan** *m*
Timor	=	**Timor** *m*
they like Cuba	=	**ils aiment Cuba**
the climate of Malta	=	**le climat de Malte**
to invade Jersey	=	**envahir Jersey**
to occupy Timor	=	**occuper Timor**

(c) Those in the third category require the inclusion of **l'île de**. Note that the English expression may be very similar.

the Isle of Man	=	**l'île de Man**

In some cases, there is a choice, especially for island groups:

the Balearics/the Balearic islands	=	**les Baléares/les îles Baléares**
the Falklands/the Falkland Islands	=	**les Malouines/les îles Malouines**
the Orkneys/the Orkney isles	=	**les Orcades/les îles Orcades**
the Comoro islands	=	**les Comores/les îles Comores**
the Seychelles	=	**les Seychelles/les îles Seychelles**

Gender of islands

As with *Towns and cities*, there is some hesitation as to whether you should say **Cuba est beau** or **Cuba est belle**. So it is safer to say: **l'île de Cuba est belle**.

In, to, and *from*

Feminine names of islands which are usually used with
the article as in type (a) above behave like the names of
countries.

Use **en** to mean *in* and *to*, and **de** to mean *from*:

to go to Sardinia	= **aller en Sardaigne**
to live in Guadeloupe	= **vivre en Guadeloupe**
to come from Corsica	= **venir de Corse**

Note the following, masculine, example:

| to go to/live in | = **aller au/vivre au Groënland** |
| Greenland | |

As elsewhere in French, **en** is rarely used with the
definite article, so that **dans le/la/les** is used when an
article is required (e.g. because there is a further
complement):

| conditions in the Corsica | = **les conditions dans la Corse de 1943** |
| of 1943 | |

With type (b) names, use **à** to mean *in* and *to* and **de** to
mean *from*:

to go to Cuba	= **aller à Cuba**
to live in Malta	= **vivre à Malte**
to come from Hawaii	= **venir d'Hawaï**

With type (c) names, use **à l'île de/aux (îles)** for *to* and *in*;
use **de l'île de/des (îles)** for *from*:

to go to the Isle of Man	= **aller à l'île de Man**
to live in the Falklands	= **vivre aux Malouines**
to come from the Antilles	= **venir des Antilles**

There is no difference in translation between *in* and *on*:

to live on Naxos	= **vivre à Naxos**
imprisoned on Saint	= **emprisonné à Sainte-Hélène**
Helena	

Exceptions

The above remarks are not exhaustive and there is some
movement in usage. Thus, recently, the traditional form **à
Haïti** has tended to be replaced by **en Haïti**, but there has
been no similar movement away from the still correct
forms **à Malte, à Jersey, à Chypre**, etc.

Jamaica	= **la Jamaïque**

This is a type (a) word, but one says:

to go to/to live in Jamaica	= **aller/vivre à la Jamaïque (en** *is unusual*).

Towns and cities

Names of French towns
Note that **Lyon** and **Marseille** do not take a final **s** in
French.

French names of British towns
Note:

London	= **Londres**
Dover	= **Douvres**
Edinburgh	= **Édimbourg**

French names of other towns
Do not forget the accent in: **Québec; Montréal**.

Note French **-bourg** for English *-burg(h)*:

Hamburg	= **Hambourg**
St Petersburg	= **Saint-Pétersbourg**

Note French **-pour** for Asian towns with *-pur/-pore* in
English:

Jaipur	=	**Jaipour**
Singapore	=	**Singapour**

Note the following North African towns:

Algiers	=	**Alger**
Tangier(s)	=	**Tanger**

The following list is not exhaustive but gives most major cities whose written name is different in French and English:

Alexandria	=	**Alexandrie**
Athens	=	**Athènes**
Barcelona	=	**Barcelone**
Brussels	=	**Bruxelles**
Cairo	=	**Le Caire**
Cape Town	=	**le Cap**
Copenhagen	=	**Copenhague**
Damascus	=	**Damas**
Frankfurt	=	**Francfort**
Geneva	=	**Genève**
Genoa	=	**Gênes**
the Hague	=	**La Haye**
Jerusalem	=	**Jérusalem**
Kabul	=	**Kaboul**
Lisbon	=	**Lisbonne**
Mexico City	=	**Mexico** (*the country is* **le Mexique**)
Moscow	=	**Moscou**
New Orleans	=	**la Nouvelle-Orléans**
Teheran	=	**Téhéran**
Venice	=	**Venise**
Vienna	=	**Vienne**
Warsaw	=	**Varsovie**

Gender of towns

Except where **le** or **la** is included, the gender of towns and cities is often unclear.

It is safest to include the word **ville**, so:

Paris is beautiful	= **la ville de Paris est belle** *or* **Paris est une belle ville**

See also *Islands*.

There are, however, certain fixed expressions which are always masculine: **le Vieux Lyon/Rouen/Strasbourg/ Marseille; le Vieil Albi; le tout Paris.**

in, to, and *from*

Use **à** for *in* and *to*, and **de** for *from*:

to live in Paris	= **vivre à Paris**
to go to Paris	= **aller à Paris**
to come from Paris	= **venir de Paris**

Where the town name includes an article, the regular compound forms are used:

to the Hague	= **à la Haye**
the Le Mans 24-hour race	= **les Vingt-quatre heures du Mans**
building at Les Arcs	= **la construction aux Arcs**
to leave from Le Havre	= **partir du Havre**

Note an increasingly common (though still sometimes frowned on) use of **sur** to mean *in and around, in the region of*:

my wife works in the Lyon area	= **ma femme travaille sur Lyon**
I travel a lot in and around Bordeaux	= **je voyage beaucoup sur Bordeaux**

Adjective forms and words for inhabitants

English has a few forms for the inhabitants of towns,

such as *Londoners, New Yorkers, Glaswegians, Parisians*, etc. French has more and these are heavily used in newspaper articles, etc. on sport. A form exists for most French, Swiss, and Belgian towns and for many in other countries:

French cities

Aix-en-Provence: aixois/e

Bordeaux: bordelais/e

Clermont-Ferrand: clermontois/e

Dijon: dijonnais/e

Grenoble: grenoblois/e

Lille: lillois/e

Limoges: limougeaud/e

Lyon: lyonnais/e

Marseille: marseillais/e

Metz: messin/e

Montpellier: montpelliérain/e

Nantes: nantais/e

Nice: niçois/e

Paris: parisien/ne

Pau: palois/e

Reims: rémois/e

Rennes: rennais/e

Rouen: rouennais/e

St Étienne: stéphanois/e

Strasbourg: strasbourgeois/e

Toulouse: toulousain/e

Tours: tourangeau/tourangelle

Versailles: versaillais/e

Belgian cities

Anvers: anversois/e

Bruxelles: bruxellois/e

Liège: liégeois/e

Canadian cities
Montréal: montréalais/e
Québec: québecois/e

Some foreign cities
Alger: algérois/e
Athènes: athénien/ne
Berlin: berlinois/e
Londres: londonien/ne
Madrid: madrilène
Moscou: moscovite
Naples: napolitain/e
New York: newyorkais/e
Pékin: pékinois/e
Rome: romain/e

Written with a capital letter the adjective forms become
nouns and are used to denote inhabitants:

she is a Parisian	= **c'est une Parisienne**
the votes of New-Yorkers	= **les voix des Newyorkais**

If there is no word, or if you do not know it, **habitant de** is
always safe:

the people of Montpellier	= **les Montpelliérains** or **les habitants de Montpellier**
the inhabitants of Nancy	= **les Nancéiens** or **les habitants de Nancy**

The adjective forms can apply to any other item:

Paris(ian) shops	= **les magasins parisiens**
New York sewers	= **les égouts newyorkais**

But do not invent adjective forms—it is almost always
safe to use constructions with **de** where English uses a
town name as a modifier:

a Bordeaux accent	= **l'accent de Bordeaux** *or* **bordelais**
Toulouse airport	= **l'aéroport de Toulouse**
the Geneva area	= **la région de Genève** *or* **genevoise**
the Angers team	= **l'équipe d'Angers** *or* **angevine**

but:

Orleans/Paris traffic	= **la circulation à Orléans/à Paris**

of

Town names in titles are also preceded by **de**:

the duke of Windsor	= **le duc de Windsor**
the archbishop of Mainz	= **l'archevêque de Mayence**

See also *Forms of address*.

to or *from*?

Note the ambiguity of **le train de Nantes**—is it coming from Nantes, or going to Nantes? To avoid ambiguity say:

to Nantes	= **à destination de Nantes**
from Nantes	= **en provenance de Nantes**

....

Oceans and seas

Here is a list of the oceans and the most important seas:

Note that **océan** and **mer** take lower-case letters; they are also preceded by the definite article, as in English:

Oceans

* the Atlantic Ocean	= **l'océan Atlantique**
the Indian Ocean	= **l'océan Indien**
* the Pacific Ocean	= **l'océan Pacifique**

Seas

the Aegean Sea	= **la mer Égée**
the Arabian Sea	= **la mer d'Arabie**

* the Baltic Sea	=	**la mer Baltique**
the Caribbean Sea	=	**la mer des Antilles**
* the Caspian Sea	=	**la mer Caspienne**
the China Sea	=	**la mer de Chine**
the Coral Sea	=	**la mer de Corail**
the Dead Sea	=	**la mer Morte**
the Ionian Sea	=	**la mer Ionienne**
the Irish Sea	=	**la mer d'Irlande**
the North Sea	=	**la mer du Nord**
the Tyrrhenian Sea	=	**la mer Tyrrhénienne**

and

the South Seas	=	**les mers du Sud**

Names with of

the Sea of Azov	=	**la mer d'Azov** (de + *town name*)
the Sea of Japan	=	**la mer du Japon** (du + *masculine country name; cp.* **du Nord**)

Like English, French sometimes drops the words **océan** or **mer**. This applies to the words marked * in the above lists. In such cases the name of the ocean or sea keeps the appropriate gender:

masculine for oceans, because **océan** is masculine

feminine for seas, because **mer** is feminine.

to swim in the Pacific	=	**se baigner dans le Pacifique**
the waters of the Caspian	=	**les eaux de la Caspienne**

But in the other cases, the abbreviated form is not possible:

the Indian Ocean	=	**l'océan Indien** (*and never* **l'Indien**)
the Aegean	=	**la mer Egée** (*and never* **l'Egée**)

This also applies to names of seas which include colours:

the Black Sea	=	**la mer Noire**

| the Red Sea | = **la mer Rouge** |
| the White Sea | = **la mer Blanche** |

Used as modifiers, the French names are usually combined with **du/de la/de l'**:

Baltic fish	= **les poissons de la Baltique**
Caspian waters	= **les eaux de la Caspienne**
Atlantic waves	= **les vagues de l'Atlantique**

Sometimes, however, other constructions are used:

| a Pacific cruise | = **une croisière dans le Pacifique** |

Lakes

Here are the names of some well-known lakes.

Note the use of lower-case **l** for **lac** and the use of the definite article:

Lake Michigan	= **le lac Michigan**
Lake Victoria	= **le lac Victoria**
the Great Salt Lake	= **le Grand Lac Salé** (*capital* **L** *here*)
Lake Geneva	= **le lac Léman** *or* **le lac de Genève**

Some lake names have **de** and some do not. The general rule is to use **de** with names which are also names of towns:

Lake Annecy	= **le lac d'Annecy**
Lake Constance	= **le lac de Constance**
Lake Como	= **le lac de Côme**

Otherwise, do not use **de**:

| Lake Erie | = **le lac Erié** |
| Lake Maggiore | = **le lac Majeur** |

For Scottish lochs and Irish loughs, keep the original title but use the definite article and a small letter:

| Loch Ness | = **le loch Ness** |
| Lough Erne | = **le lough Erne** |

English occasionally drops the word *Lake*; in French it is safest to keep the word **lac**:

| a campsite near Balaton | = **un camping près du lac Balaton** |
| the falls between Erie and Ontario | = **les chutes entre le lac Erié et le lac Ontario** |

Lake names used as modifiers keep the **le** (which of course becomes **du** when combined with **de**):

| Lake Huron waters | = **les eaux du lac Huron** |
| Lake Chad fishermen | = **les pêcheurs du lac Tchad** |

....

Rivers

There is an important difference in French between certain major rivers, referred to as **fleuves** (technically, those which flow into a sea) and the rest, referred to as **rivières** (technically, those which flow into a **fleuve**). There are also general expressions for both such as **cours d'eau**.

Here are the names of all the French and the major non-French **fleuves**:

French *fleuves*

The most important ones are:

la Garonne, la Loire, la Seine, le Rhin, le Rhône

Among the smaller ones, note **la Somme, le Var** etc.

Non-French *fleuves*:

| the Amazon | = **l'Amazone** *m* |

the Congo	=	**le Congo**
the Danube	=	**le Danube**
the Dnieper	=	**le Dniepr**
the Ganges	=	**le Gange**
the Indus	=	**l'Indus** *m*
the Mississippi	=	**le Mississippi**
the Niger	=	**le Niger**
the Nile	=	**le Nil**
the Po	=	**le Po**
the Saint Lawrence	=	**le Saint-Laurent**
the Tagus	=	**le Tage**
the Thames	=	**la Tamise**
the Volga	=	**la Volga**
the Zambezi	=	**le Zambèze**

Use the definite article when referring to rivers, as in English:

we crossed the Orne	=	**nous avons traversé l'Orne**
it has polluted the Thames	=	**cela a pollué la Tamise**
their windows give onto the Rhone	=	**leurs fenêtres donnent sur le Rhône**
to swim in the Garonne	=	**se baigner dans la Garonne**

French cannot use an equivalent for English *river*:

| the river Thames | = | **la Tamise** |
| the Potomac river | = | **le Potomac** |

But there are a few cases where **Fleuve** is part of the name (i.e. where there is no 'real' proper noun):

| the Yellow River | = | **le Fleuve Jaune** |

Used as modifiers, river names are normally preceded in French by **du/de la/de l'**:

the Seine estuary	=	l'estuaire de la Seine
Danube waters	=	les eaux du Danube
the Rhine quayside	=	les quais du Rhin
the Nile delta	=	le delta du Nil

....

Points of the compass

The cardinal points are normally listed in the same order in French as in English; French prefers a small letter for the name while English uses a capital letter. Both languages use capital letters for the abbreviated forms:

North	=	nord (N)
South	=	sud (S)
East	=	est (E)
West	=	ouest (O)

Compound directions also use the same order as in English; French inserts an extra hyphen:

northeast	=	nord-est (NE)
southwest	=	sud-ouest (SO)
north-northeast	=	nord-nord-est (NNE)
south-southwest	=	sud-sud-ouest (SSO)

Note the use of **quart** to translate *by*:

southwest by south	=	sud-ouest quart sud

A capital letter is, however, used in French if the word refers to a region. In such cases the direction word is always masculine:

to live in the North	=	vivre dans le Nord
the North of Scotland	=	le Nord de l'Écosse

Be careful to distinguish:

to the North of Spain	=	au nord de l'Espagne (*i.e. further North*)

| due north of here | = **droit au nord** |

and:

| in the North of Spain | = **dans le Nord de l'Espagne** |

But **au nord** by itself can mean *in the north* or *to the north*.

Both *the North of* and *northern* are usually **le Nord** in French:

| the northern parts of Japan | = **le Nord du Japon** |
| Eastern France | = **l'Est de la France** |

Compass points as adverbs

When movement or headings are concerned it is usually safe to use **vers le**:

| to move West | = **se déplacer vers l'ouest** |

Similar translations work for derived words indicating direction:

to go northwards	= **aller vers le nord**
to head in a northerly direction	= **se diriger vers le nord**
a northbound ship	= **un bateau qui se dirige vers le nord**

When fixed places are concerned **au X de** is usual:

| it is seven miles north of the town | = **c'est à dix kilomètres au nord de la ville** |

Note also:

| the windows face south | = **les fenêtres donnent au sud** *or* **sont orientées au sud** |

Compass points as adjectives
Winds

Note the use of **de** in the following:

the north wind	=	**le vent de nord**
south-west winds	=	**des vents de sud-ouest**
a southerly (wind)	=	**un vent de sud**
prevailing southerlies	=	**des vents dominants de sud**

But:

the wind is in the south	=	**le vent est au sud**

Other cases

Normally the French words are used without preceding
de/du and are invariable:

the south coast	=	**la côte sud**
the north door	=	**la porte nord**
the west face (of a mountain)	=	**la face ouest**

northerner, westerner

There are a number of translations for these words,
depending on the context:

Westerners/Easterners

(*people from a Western/* *Eastern region*)	=	**les gens de l'ouest/de l'est**
(*people of Western/* *Eastern culture*)	=	**les Occidentaux/les Orientaux**

Northerners/Southerners

(*people of the* *appropriate region*)	=	**les gens du nord/du sud**
(*sides in the American* *Civil War*)	=	**les Nordistes/les Sudistes**

There is no overall pattern for compound place names
such as *the Wild West*; *the Far East*; or for *East Prussia*;
South Africa; *North Yemen*.

Weather

Here are some of the main weather words:

Nouns

cloud	= **nuage** *m*
fog	= **brouillard** *m*
hail	= **grêle** *f*
hurricane	= **ouragan** *m*
lightning	= **foudre** *f*
mist	= **brume** *f*
rain	= **pluie** *f*
sleet	= **neige** *f* **fondue**
snow	= **neige** *f*
storm (*i.e. wind and rain or snow*)	= **tempête** *f*
the sun	= **soleil** *m*
thunder	= **tonnerre** *m*
thunderstorm	= **orage** *m*
tornado	= **tornade** *f*
wind	= **vent** *m*

Verbs

to rain	= **pleuvoir**
to snow	= **neiger**
to hail	= **grêler**
to sleet: it is sleeting	= **il tombe de la neige fondue**
to thunder	= **tonner**

Expressions

Since *weather* = **le temps**, we get:

fine weather	= **le beau temps**

| bad weather | = **le mauvais temps** |

etc.

With the verb **faire, temps** can be dropped:

| it is fine *or* the weather is fine | = **il fait beau temps** *or* **il fait beau** |
| the weather is bad | = **il fait mauvais temps** *or* **il fait mauvais** |

Words in -y

Note how it is —y is translated by **il y a du/de la** — *or* **il fait du/de la** — in the following:

it is sunny	= **il y a du soleil** *or* **il fait du soleil**
it is foggy	= **il y a du brouillard**
it is misty	= **il y a de la brume**
it is windy	= **il y a du vent** *or* **il fait du vent**

French has many adjectives ending **-eux/-euse. The** following examples attempt to give some guidelines of when they can and cannot be used:

cloudy	= **nuageux/-euse**
a cloudy sky	= **un ciel nuageux**
cloudy weather	= **un temps nuageux**
rainy	= **pluvieux/-euse**
rainy weather	= **un temps pluvieux**
the rainy season	= **la saison des pluies**
misty	= **brumeux/-euse**
a misty landscape	= **un paysage brumeux**
misty weather	= **un temps brumeux**
sunny	= **ensoleillé/-e**
a sunny sky	= **un ciel ensoleillé**

sunny weather	= **un temps ensoleillé**
thundery	= **orageux/-euse**
thundery weather	= **un temps orageux**
a thundery sky	= **un ciel d'orage**

Use of expressions in the plural

French (like English) sometimes uses plural expressions meaning *a season of…/an area of…*:

torrential rain	= **des pluies diluviennes**
the recent rains	= **les dernières pluies**
heavy/light rain	= **de fortes/de petites pluies**
the melting of the snow(s)	= **la fonte des neiges**
the eternal snows near the peak	= **les neiges éternelles près du sommet**

(See also compound words translated with **des neiges** below.)

morning mist(s)	= **des brumes matinales**

Translating expressions with *in*

The translation varies according to the item and the exact sense. The main point to remember is that **dans** is extremely rare:

to stay in the sun	= **rester au soleil**
right in the sun/in full sunlight	= **en plein soleil**
to flap around in the wind	= **flotter au vent**

sous is usual with **un soleil** + adjective:

to walk in the burning sun	= **se promener sous un soleil brûlant**
to work in bright sunlight	= **travailler sous un soleil éclatant** *or* **radieux**

Note also:

beneath a leaden sky = **sous un ciel de plomb**

sous is also common with falling rain, snow, etc.:

to walk in the rain = **se promener sous la pluie**

I was singing in the rain = **je chantais sous la pluie**

a walk in the snow = **une promenade dans la neige** (*if it is on the ground*) *or* **sous la neige** (*if it is falling*)

they went on walking in/through the thunderstorm = **ils ont continué à marcher sous l'orage**

Translating English compounds

In many cases, constructions with **de pluie/neige** etc. can be used; these are often no different from English ones using *of*:

fog bank *or* bank of fog = **banc** *m* **de brume**

foglamp = **feu** *m* **de brouillard**

hailstorm = **averse** *f* **de grêle**

moonlight = **clair** *m* **de lune**

raindrop *or* drop of rain = **goutte** *f* **de pluie**

rainwear = **vêtements** *mpl* **de pluie**

snowflake = **flocon** *m* **de neige**

snowstorm = **tempête** *f* **de neige**

storm warning = **avis** *m* **de tempête**

thunder clap *or* clap of thunder = **coup** *m* **de tonnerre**

More rarely, **du/de la/des** occur rather than **de**:

snowmobile = **scooter** *m* **des neiges**

sunlight = **lumière** *f* **du soleil**

And expressions with adjectives also occur:

cloud cover	=	**couverture** *f* **nuageuse**
stormcloud	=	**nuage** *m* **orageux**

Sometimes French also uses compound words, and the weather word tends to come second:

snowplough	=	**chasse-neige** *m inv*
storm lantern	=	**lampe-tempête** *f*

Or, French may use a Latin or Greek element to combine with the other item:

rain gauge	=	**pluviomètre** *m*

Sometimes there is a simple lexical item equivalent to the English compound one:

hailstone	=	**grêlon** *m*
raincoat	=	**imperméable** *m*
snowdrift	=	**congère** *f*
snowshoes	=	**raquettes** *fpl*
sunstroke	=	**insolation** *f*
showerproof	=	**imperméabilisé**

See also *Temperature*.

Quantities and measurements

The use of *de* in measurements

The preposition **de** is particularly problematic in expressions of measurements. It is used in the following:

- in questions corresponding to the English *how*:

how long is the rope?	=	**de quelle longueur est la corde?**
how high is the tower?	=	**de quelle hauteur est la tour?**
how wide is the river?	=	**de quelle largeur est la rivière?**

but note:

how deep is the river?	=	**quelle est la profondeur de la rivière?**
how big is your garden?	=	**quelle est la superficie de votre jardin?**
how big is the tank?	=	**quel est le volume du réservoir?**
how high is the plane?	=	**quelle est l'altitude de l'avion?** *or* **à quelle altitude est l'avion?**
how fast does the car go?	=	**quelle est la vitesse de la voiture?** *or* **à quelle vitesse la voiture roule-t-elle?**
how hot is the milk?	=	**quelle est la température du lait?** *or* **à quelle température le lait est-il?**
how far is the village?	=	**à quelle distance se trouve le village?**
how tall is the thief?	=	**quelle est la taille du voleur?** *or* **combien mesure le voleur?**
how heavy is the baby?	=	**quel est le poids du bébé?** *or* **combien pèse le bébé?**
how much does the house cost?	=	**quel est le prix de la maison?** *or* **combien coûte la maison?**

- in the following constructions with the verb **faire**:

what is its length?	=	**combien fait-il de longueur?**
what is its height?	=	**combien fait-il de hauteur?**
what is its volume?	=	**combien fait-il de volume?**
it is ten metres long	=	**elle fait dix mètres de long**
it is twenty metres high	=	**elle fait vingt mètres de hauteur** *or* **de haut**
it is ten metres deep	=	**elle fait dix mètres de profondeur** *or* **de profond**
it is ten square metres	=	**elle fait dix mètres carrés de surface** *or* **de superficie**
it is ten centimetres too long	=	**il fait dix centimètres de trop**
he is three centimetres shorter than she is	=	**il fait trois centimètres de moins qu'elle**

- when the measurement follows the verb **être**:

its length/width/depth is ten metres	=	**sa longueur/largeur/profondeur est de dix mètres**
its volume is ten litres	=	**son volume est de dix litres**
its altitude is 5,000 metres	=	**son altitude est de 5 000 mètres**
its capacity is 200 litres	=	**sa contenance est de 200 litres**
its speed was 200 kilometres an hour	=	**sa vitesse était de 200 km/h**
the distance from A to B is two kilometres	=	**la distance entre A et B est de deux kilomètres**

- similarly:

C and D are the same size	=	**C est de la même taille que D** *or* **C et D sont de la même taille**
C and D are the same height	=	**C est de la même hauteur que D** *or* **C et D sont de la même hauteur**
C and D are the same width	=	**C et D sont de la même largeur** *or* **C est de la même largeur que D**

- when the measurement is of excess or shortfall (note the word order):

it is three metres too short	= **il est trop court de trois mètres**
it is three kilometres too far	= **il est trop loin de trois kilomètres**

● when the measurement is an attribute of the noun (often a compound adjective in English):

a 200-cubic-metre tank	= **un réservoir de 200 mètres cubes**
a rope ten metres long	= **une corde de dix mètres (de long)**
an athlete more than six feet tall	≈ **un athlète de plus d'un mètre quatre-vingts**
a tower over a hundred metres in height	= **une tour de plus de cent mètres (de hauteur)**
a ten-kilometre walk	= **une promenade de dix kilomètres**
a 200-square-metre plot	= **un terrain de 200 mètres carrés**
a 200-litre tank	= **un réservoir de 200 litres**

● Note also:

at a height of twenty metres	= **à une hauteur de vingt mètres** *or* **à vingt mètres de hauteur**
at an altitude of 5,000 metres	= **à une altitude de 5 000 mètres** *or* **à 5 000 mètres d'altitude**
at a distance of two kilometres	= **à une distance de deux kilomètres** *or* **à deux kilomètres de distance**
at a depth of seven metres	= **à une profondeur de sept mètres** *or* **à sept mètres de profondeur**

Similarly: **une longueur de trois centimètres, un volume de cinq mètres cubes, une surface de 200 mètres carrés, un poids de deux cent tonnes, une vitesse de cent quatre-vingt kilomètres à l'heure, une température de 37°.**

● after **plus** or **moins**, translating *more, less, over, under*, etc.:

over 200 cubic metres	= **plus de 200 mètres cube**
less than two metres	= **moins de deux mètres**
more than 200 kilometres an hour	= **plus de 200 km/h**

etc.

Numbers

Cardinal numbers in French

0	zéro*	71	soixante et onze, septante et un (etc)
1	un	72	soixante-douze
2	deux	73	soixante-treize
3	trois	74	soixante-quatorze
4	quatre	75	soixante-quinze
5	cinq	76	soixante-seize
6	six	77	soixante-dix-sept
7	sept	78	soixante-dix-huit
8	huit	79	soixante-dix-neuf
9	neuf	80	quatre-vingts‡
10	dix	81	quatre-vingt-un§
11	onze	82	quatre-vingt-deux
12	douze	90	quatre-vingt-dix, nonante (in Belgium, Canada, Switzerland etc.)
13	treize	91	quatre-vingt-onze, nonante et un
14	quatorze	92	quatre-vingt-douze, nonante-deux (etc)
15	quinze	99	quatre-vingt-dix-neuf
16	seize	100	cent
17	dix-sept	101	cent un
18	dix-huit	102	cent deux
19	dix-neuf	110	cent dix
20	vingt	111	cent onze
21	vingt et un	112	cent douze
22	vingt-deux	187	cent quatre-vingt-sept
30	trente	200	deux cents
31	trente et un	250	deux cent¶ cinquante
32	trente-deux	300	trois cents
40	quarante	1 000‖	mille
50	cinquante	1 001	mille un
60	soixante		
70	soixante-dix, septante (in Belgium, Canada Switzerland etc.)		

1 002	mille deux	102 000	cent deux mille
1 020	mille vingt	1 000 000	million‡‡
1 200	mille deux cents	1 264 932	un million deux
2 000	deux mille††		cent soixante-
10 000	dix mille		quatre mille neuf
10 200	dix mille deux cents		cent trente deux
100 000	cent mille	1 000 000 000	un milliard‡‡

* In English 0 may be called nought, zero or even nothing; French is always zéro; a nought = un zéro.

‡ Also huitante in Switzerland. Note that when 80 is used as a page number it has no s, e.g. page eighty = page quatre-vingt.

§ Note that vingt has no s when it is in the middle of a number. The only exception to this rule is when quatre-vingts is followed by millions, milliards or billions, e.g. quatre-vingts millions, quatre-vingts billions etc.

¶ Note that cent does not take an s when it is in the middle of a number. The only exception to this rule is when it is followed by millions, milliards or billions, e.g. trois cents millions, six cents billions etc. It has a normal plural when it modifies other nouns, e.g. 200 inhabitants = deux cents habitants.

|| Note that figures in French are set out differently; where English would have a comma, French has simply a space. It is also possible in French to use a full stop (period) here, e.g. 1.000. French, like English, writes dates without any separation between thousands and hundreds, e.g. in 1995 = en 1995.

†† Mille is invariable; it never takes an s.

‡‡ Note that the French words million, milliard and billion are nouns, and when written out in full they take de before another noun, e.g. a million inhabitants is un million d'habitants, a billion francs is un billion de francs. However, when written in figures, 1,000,000 inhabitants is 1 000 000 habitants, but is still spoken as un million d'habitants. When million etc. is part of a complex number, de is not used before the nouns, e.g. 6,000,210 people = six millions deux cent dix personnes.

How to write numbers

Where English has a decimal point, French has a comma:

  16.2   = **16,2**

The English comma in large numbers corresponds to a full stop in French:

  3,257,422   = **3.257.422**

How to say numbers

Numbers with a decimal point in English have a comma in French and are normally said like this: **16,2 = seize virgule deux**. In some cases, it is also possible to say **seize deux**.

When such a number is accompanied by a unit of measurement, like **mètre, litre**, etc., there are three ways of saying it:

16,2 m can be **seize virgule deux mètres, seize mètres virgule deux**, or more colloquially **seize mètres deux**.

Use of *de* with *million* and *milliard*

  a million pounds   = **un million de livres**
  a milliard centimes = **un milliard de centimes**

Phrases

  numbers up to ten   = **les nombres jusqu'à dix**
  I can count up to ten = **je sais compter jusqu'à dix**
  all ten boys   = **les dix garçons**
  all ten of them   = **tous les dix**

Note the word order in the following:

  the first two   = **les deux premiers/premières**
  the last three   = **les trois derniers/dernières**

my last ten pounds	= **mes dix dernières livres**
the next twelve weeks	= **les douze prochaines semaines** or **les douze semaines à venir**

Similarly:

the other two	= **les deux autres**

Approximate numbers

environ can always be used.

there are about six apples	= **il y a environ six pommes**
there are about ten	= **il y en a environ dix**

However, French also has some special words ending in **-aine**:

about ten	= **une dizaine**
about twelve	= **une douzaine** (note that **une douzaine** can also mean a dozen/*exactly twelve*, as in **une douzaine d'œufs**)
about fifteen	= **une quinzaine**
about twenty	= **une vingtaine**

Similarly, **une trentaine, une quarantaine, une cinquantaine, une soixantaine** and **une centaine**. Do not use **-aine** words for other numbers.

For *about a thousand*, use **millier + de**:

several thousand books	= **plusieurs milliers de livres**

Note the use of **de** with the **-aine** words:

about ten books	= **une dizaine de livres**
about twelve people	= **une douzaine de personnes**
about fifteen kilometres	= **une quinzaine de kilomètres**

Note also:

there are at least ten = **il y a une bonne dizaine de livres**
books

there are about twenty = **il y en a une vingtaine**

Calculations

$22 + 7 = 29$: *say* **vingt-deux et sept font vingt-neuf**, *or* **vingt-deux plus sept égale vingt-neuf**

$22 - 7 = 15$: *say* **vingt-deux moins sept font quinze**, *or* **vingt-deux moins sept égale quinze**, *or* **sept ôtés de vingt-deux font quinze**

$22 \times 7 = 154$: *say* **vingt-deux fois sept font cent cinquante-quatre**, *or* **vingt-deux fois sept égale cent cinquante-quatre**

$28 : 7 = 4$: *say* **vingt-huit divisés par sept font quatre**, *or* **vingt-huit divisé par sept égale quatre**

Note also the pronunciation of:

7^2: *say* **sept au carré**, *or* **sept puissance deux**

7^3: *say* **sept puissance trois**

7^4: *say* **sept puissance quatre**

etc.

$\sqrt{9}$: *say* **racine de neuf**, *or* **racine carrée de neuf**

Decimals in French

Note that French uses a comma where English has a decimal point.

	say
0,25	**zéro virgule vingt-cinq**
0,05	**zéro virgule zéro cinq**
0,75	**zéro virgule soixante-quinze**
3,45	**trois virgule quarante-cinq**
8,195	**huit virgule cent quatre-vingt-quinze**
9,1567	**neuf virgule quinze cent soixante-sept**
9,3456	**neuf virgule trois mille quatre cent cinquante-six**

Percentages in French

	say
	say
25%	**vingt-cinq pour cent**
50%	**cinquante pour cent**
100%	**cent pour cent**
200%	**deux cents pour cent**
365%	**troix cent soixante-cinq pour cent**
4,25%	**quatre virgule vingt-cinq pour cent**

Fractions in French

say

$\frac{1}{2}$ **un demi**
Note that half, *when not a fraction, is translated by the noun* moitié *or the adjective* demi.

$\frac{1}{3}$ **un tiers**

$\frac{1}{4}$ **un quart**

$\frac{1}{5}$ **un cinquième**

$\frac{1}{6}$ **un sixième**

$\frac{1}{10}$ **un dixième**

$\frac{1}{2}$ **un douzième (etc.)**

$\frac{2}{3}$ **deux tiers**
Note the use of les *and* d'entre *when these fractions are used about a group of people or things:* two-thirds of them = les deux tiers d'entre eux.

$\frac{2}{5}$ **deux cinquièmes**

$\frac{2}{10}$ **deux dixièmes (etc.)**

$\frac{3}{4}$ **trois quarts**

$\frac{3}{5}$ **trois cinquièmes**

$\frac{3}{10}$ **trois dixièmes (etc.)**

$1\frac{1}{2}$ **un et demi**

$1\frac{1}{4}$ **un et quart**

$1\frac{1}{5}$ **un (et) un cinquième**

$1\frac{1}{6}$ **un (et) un sixième**

$1\frac{1}{7}$ un (et) un septième (etc.)

$5\frac{2}{3}$ cinq (et) deux tiers

$5\frac{3}{4}$ cinq (et) trois quarts

$5\frac{4}{5}$ cinq (et) quatre cinquièmes

$\frac{45}{100}$ ths of a second

         quarante-cinq centièmes de seconde

All the other abbreviations of ordinal numbers are invariable.

Ordinal numbers in French[§]		
1st	1er[‡]	premier (*feminine* première)
2nd	2e	second *or* deuxième
3rd	3e	troisième
4th	4e	quatrième
5th	5e	cinquième
6th	6e	sixième
7th	7e	septième
8th	8e	huitième
9th	9e	neuvième
10th	10e	dixième
20th	20e	vingtième
21st	21e	vingt et unième
22nd	22e	vingt-deuxième
23rd	23e	vingt-troisième
24th	24e	vingt-quatrième
25th	25e	vingt-cinquième
30th	30e	trentième
31st	31e	trente et unième
40th	40e	quarantième

50th	50°	cinquantième
60th	60°	soixantième
70th	70°	soixante-dixième, septantième (in Belgium, Canada, Switzerland etc.)
71st	71°	soixante et onzième, septante et unième (etc.)
72nd	72°	soixante-douzième
73rd	73°	soixante-treizième
74th	74°	soixante-quatorzième
75th	75°	soixante-quinzième
76th	76°	soixante-seizième
77th	77°	soixante-dix-septième
78th	78°	soixante-dix-huitième
79th	79°	soixante-dix-neuvième
80th	80°	quatre-vingtième
81st	81°	quatre-vingt-unième
90th	90°	quatre-vingt-dixième, nonantième (in Belgium, Canada, Switzerland etc.)
91st	91°	quatre-vingt-onzième nonante et unième (etc.)
99th	99°	quatre-vingt-dix-neuvième
100th	100°	centième
101st	101°	cent unième
102nd	102°	cent deuxième
196th	196°	cent quatre-vingt-seizième
200th	200°	deux centième
300th	300°	trois centième
1,000th	1 000°	millième
2,000th	2 000°	deux millième
1,000,000th	1 000 000° millionième

---

§ *All the ordinal numbers in French behave like ordinary adjectives and take normal plural endings where appropriate.*

‡ *This is the masculine form; the feminine is 1re and the plural 1ers (m) or 1res (f).*

Note the special use of **premier** in:

| King James the first | = | **le roi Jacques Ier** (*say* **Jacques premier**) |

but:

| King James the second | = | **le roi Jacques II** (*say* **Jacques deux**) |
| Napoleon the third | = | **Napoléon III** (*say* **Napoléon trois**) |

etc.

| the first of May | = | **le premier mai** |

but:

| the second of May | = | **le deux mai** |
| the third of May | = | **le trois mai** |

etc.

See also *Dates*.

Classifications

the first in the morning	=	**le premier/la première/les premiers/ les premières de la matinée**
the second in Europe	=	**le deuxième/la deuxième/les deuxièmes en Europe**
the third in the world	=	**le troisième/la troisième/les troisièmes au monde**
the third richest country in the world	=	**le troisième pays le plus riche du monde**

....

Collectives and quantities

Collectives

Most collective expressions in French use **de** with no article:

a lot of people	= **beaucoup de gens**
few ministers	= **peu de ministres**
a good number of guests	= **bon nombre d'invités**

This also applies to expressions such as:

a mass of applicants	= **une multitude de candidats**
masses of dictionaries	= **des piles de dictionnaires**
tons of food	= **des tonnes de nourriture**
crowds of spectators	= **des foules de spectateurs**
a flock of sheep	= **un troupeau de moutons**
herds of holidaymakers	= **des troupeaux de vacanciers**

But French uses **du/de la/de l'/des** after **la plupart, la majorité,** and **bien**:

most cars	= **la plupart des voitures**
most people	= **la majorité des gens**
most of the time	= **la plupart du temps**
many times	= **bien des fois**

Compare:

a majority of people	= **une majorité de gens**
the majority of people	= **la majorité des gens**

Note also:

most of the wine	= **presque tout le vin**

Singular or plural verb?

Collective expressions are more often singular in French than they are in English, and usually there is no choice:

the police wishes *or* wish to speak to you	= **la police veut te parler**
the government has *or* have decided	= **le gouvernement a décidé**
the team has *or* have succeeded	= **l'équipe a réussi**

French prefers a singular verb after **la majorité** and **une minorité**:

the major part of the books remained unsold	=	**la majorité des livres est restée invendue**
a minority of people think so	=	**une minorité de gens le pense** (*or* **le pensent**)

But the plural is used after **la plupart des, bon nombre de,** etc.:

most teachers retire as soon as they can	=	**la plupart des enseignants partent à la retraite dès qu'ils le peuvent**
lots of people drink wine	=	**bon nombre de gens boivent du vin**

Quantities

The use of *en*

Note the use of **en** when the thing you are talking about is understood but not expressed. Note also the position of **en**.

there is/are a lot	=	**il y en a beaucoup**
there are lots of them	=	**il y en a beaucoup**
I've got a lot	=	**j'en ai beaucoup**
I haven't got a lot	=	**je n'en ai pas beaucoup**
there are several	=	**il y en a plusieurs**
I've got five litres	=	**j'en ai cinq litres**
I bought two pounds	=	**j'en ai acheté deux livres**
I've seen six	=	**j'en ai vu six**

More or less

Alan has got more apples than Bob	=	**Alan a plus de pommes que Bob**
Alan has got more than Bob	=	**Alan en a plus que Bob**
Bob has got fewer apples than Alan	=	**Bob a moins de pommes qu'Alan**

Bob has got fewer than Alan	=	**Bob en a moins qu'Alan**
Alan hasn't got as many apples as Bob	=	**Alan n'a pas autant de pommes que Bob**
Alan hasn't got as many as Bob	=	**Alan n'en a pas autant que Bob**

Similarly with all kinds of words (*sugar, money, courage,* etc.).

much more than	=	**beaucoup plus que**
a little more than	=	**un peu plus que**
much less than	=	**beaucoup moins que**
a little less than	=	**un peu moins que**
a few more people than yesterday	=	**quelques personnes de plus qu'hier**

Note the use of **de** in the following:

there are more than ten books	=	**il y a plus de dix livres**
there are fewer than ten apples	=	**il y a moins de dix pommes**
there are more than ten	=	**il y en a plus de dix**
there are fewer than ten	=	**il y en a moins de dix**
he takes more sugar than me	=	**il met plus de sucre que moi**

Relative numbers

there are five apples to the kilo	=	**il y a cinq pommes au kilo**
there are five to the kilo	=	**il y en a cinq au kilo**
you get five for ten francs	=	**il y en a cinq pour dix francs**
you get six glasses to the bottle	=	**il y a six verres par bouteille**

See also *Currencies and money*.

Note that the French calculate the petrol consumption of vehicles in litres per 100 km:

it does 28 miles to the gallon ≈ **elle fait dix litres aux cent**

....

Volume

Volume measurement

Note that French has a comma where English has a decimal point.

1 cu in = **16,38 cm³**
1 cu ft = **0,03 m³**
1 cu yd = **0,76 m³**

There are three ways of saying **16,38 cm3**, and other measurements like it: **seize virgule trente-huit centimètres cubes** or (less formally) **seize centimètres cubes virgule trente-huit** or **seize centimètres cubes trente-huit.**

For how to say numbers in French, see *Numbers.*

QUESTIONS

what is the volume of the container?	= **quel est le volume du conteneur?**
what is its volume?	= **quel est son volume?** *or* **quel volume fait-il/elle?** *or* **combien fait-il/elle de volume?**

For the use of **de**, see *The use of* de *in measurements.*

ANSWERS

its volume is 200 cubic metres	= **il/elle fait 200 mètres cubes**
it's one metre by two metres by three metres	= **il/elle fait un mètre sur deux mètres sur trois mètres**

COMPARISONS

this heap is of greater volume than that one	= ce tas-ci fait plus de volume que ce tas-là *or* le volume de ce tas-ci est supérieur à celui de ce tas-là
this box is of smaller volume than that box	= cette boîte-ci fait moins de volume que cette boîte-là *or* le volume de cette boîte-ci est inférieur à celui de cette boîte-là
tube A has the same volume as tube B	= le tube A fait le même volume que le tube B *or* le tube A et le tube B font le même volume *or* le tube A et le tube B ont le même volume

OTHER PHRASES

a million cubic centimetres make one cubic metre	= un million de centimètres cubes font un mètre cube
a 1,500 cc engine	= un moteur de 1500 cm³ (*say* centimètres cubes)
sold by the cubic metre	= vendu au mètre cube

....

Measurements of length, height, etc.

Note that French has a comma where English has a decimal point.

1 in = **2,54 cm*** (**centimètres**)
1 ft = **30,48 cm**
1 yd = **91,44 cm**
1 furlong = **201,17 m** (**mètres**)
1 ml = **1,61 km** (**kilomètres**)

*There are three ways of saying **2,54 cm**, and other measurements like it: **deux virgule cinquante-quatre centimètres,** or (less formally) **deux centimètres virgule cinquante-quatre,** or **deux centimètres cinquante-quatre.**

For how to say numbers in French, see *Numbers*.

Length

Note the use of **de** in many of the following examples.

QUESTIONS

| how long is the rope? | = **de quelle longueur est la corde?** |

For the use of **de**, see *The use of* de *in measurements*.

ANSWERS

| it's ten metres long | = **elle est longue de dix mètres** *or* **elle fait dix mètres (de long)** |
| its length is ten metres | = **sa longueur est de dix mètres** |

COMPARISONS

this rope is longer than that rope	= **cette corde-ci est plus longue que cette corde-là**
that rope is shorter than this rope	= **cette corde-là est plus courte que cette corde-ci** *or* **cette corde-là est moins longue que cette corde-ci**
the sofa is as long as the carpet	= **le canapé est aussi long que le tapis**
the sofa is the same length as the carpet	= **le canapé a la même longueur que le tapis** *or* **le canapé est de la même longueur que le tapis**
the sofa and the carpet are the same length	= **le canapé et le tapis ont la même longueur** *or* **le canapé et le tapis sont de la même longueur**
it's three metres too short	= **il est trop court de trois mètres**
it's three metres too long	= **il est trop long de trois mètres** *or* **il fait trois mètres de trop**

OTHER PHRASES

ten decimetres make one metre	= **dix décimètres font un mètre**
a 12-foot snake	≈ **un serpent de 3,60 m**
sold by the metre	= **vendu au mètre**

| six metres of silk | = | **six mètres de soie** |
| ten metres of rope | = | **dix mètres de corde** |

See also *Currencies and money*.

Height
People
QUESTIONS

| how tall is he? | = | **combien mesure-t-il?** *or* **quelle est sa taille?** |

ANSWERS

| he's six feet tall | = | **il mesure un mètre quatre-vingts** *or* **il fait un mètre quatre-vingts** |

COMPARISONS

Alan is taller than Bob	=	**Alan est plus grand que Bob**
Bob is shorter than Alan	=	**Bob est plus petit que Alan** *or* **Bob est moins grand que Alan**
Chris is as tall as Diana	=	**Chris est aussi grand que Diana**
Chris is the same height as Diana	=	**Chris a la même taille que Diana** *or* **Chris est de la même taille que Diana**

For the use of **de**, see *The use of de in measurements*.

Chris and Diana are the same height	=	**Chris et Diana ont la même taille** *or* **Chris et Diana sont de la même taille**
he is three centimetres too short	=	**il est trop petit de trois centimètres** *or* **il lui manque trois centimètres**
he is three centimetres too tall	=	**il est trop grand de trois centimètres** *or* **il fait trois centimètres de trop**
he is three centimetres shorter than she is	=	**il fait trois centimètres de moins qu'elle**

OTHER PHRASES

| a six-foot-tall athlete | = | **un athlète d'un mètre quatre-vingts** |

an athlete over six feet in height	= **un athlète de plus d'un mètre quatre-vingts**

Things

QUESTIONS

how high is the tower?	= **quelle est la hauteur de la tour?** or **de quelle hauteur est la tour?** or **combien mesure la tour?**

For the use of **de**, see *The use of* de *in measurements*.

ANSWERS

it's twenty metres	= **elle mesure vingt mètres** or **elle fait vingt mètres (de haut/de hauteur)**
its height is twenty metres	= **sa hauteur est de vingt mètres**

COMPARISONS

the tower is higher than the house	= **la tour est plus haute que la maison**
the house is lower than the tower	= **la maison est plus basse que la tour** or **la maison est moins haute que la tour**
the tower is as high as the castle	= **la tour est aussi haute que le château**
the tower is the same height as the castle	= **la tour a la même hauteur que le château** or **la tour est de la même hauteur que le château**
the tower and the castle are the same height	= **la tour et le château ont la même hauteur** or **la tour et le château sont de la même hauteur**
it is three metres too low	= **elle est trop basse de trois mètres**
it is three metres too high	= **elle est trop haute de trois mètres** or **elle fait trois mètres de trop (en hauteur)**

OTHER PHRASES

a 100-metre-high tower	= **une tour de cent mètres (de hauteur/de haut)**

a tower over 100 metres in height	= **une tour de plus de cent mètres (de hauteur/de haut)**

Altitude

QUESTIONS

how high is the plane?	= **à quelle altitude est l'avion?** or **à quelle altitude l'avion vole-t-il?**

(Note that in this case French uses **à**, not **de**.)

ANSWERS

it is flying at 5,000 metres	= **il vole à 5 000 mètres** or **il vole à 5 000 mètres d'altitude** or **il vole à une altitude de 5 000 mètres**

For the use of **de**, see *The use of* de *in measurements*.

it is flying at an altitude of over 5,000 metres	= **il vole à plus de 5 000 mètres** or **il vole à plus de 5 000 mètres d'altitude** or **il vole à une altitude de plus de 5 000 mètres**
its altitude is 5,000 metres	= **son altitude est de 5 000 mètres**

COMPARISONS

the jet is flying higher than the small plane	= **le jet vole plus haut que le petit avion**
the small plane is flying lower than the jet	= **le petit avion vole plus bas que le jet**
the big plane is flying at the same altitude as the small one	= **le gros avion vole à la même altitude que le petit avion**
the big plane and the small one are flying at the same altitude	= **le gros avion et le petit avion volent à la même altitude**

Distance

QUESTIONS

what's the distance from Aberdeen to Brussels?	= **quelle distance y a-t-il entre Aberdeen et Bruxelles?**
how far is it from Aberdeen to Brussels?	= **à quelle distance Aberdeen est-il de Bruxelles?**

ANSWERS

it's 1,000 kilometres	= **il y a mille kilomètres**
the village is two kilometres away	= **le village est à deux kilomètres (de distance)**
the distance between Aberdeen and Brussels is 1,000 kilometres	= **la distance entre Aberdeen et Bruxelles est de mille kilomètres**

For the use of **de**, see *The use of* de *in measurements*.

OTHER PHRASES

at a distance of two kilometres	= **à une distance de deux kilomètres**
a village two kilometres away	= **un village à deux kilomètres**

COMPARISONS

Contrast **que** and **de** in the following:

A is nearer than B	= **A est plus près que B**
A is nearer to B	= **A est plus près de B**
B is further than A	= **B est plus loin que A** *or* **B est moins près que A**
C is nearer to B than A is	= **C est plus près de B que A**
A is nearer to B than to C	= **A est plus près de B que de C**
A is as far as B	= **A est aussi loin que B**
A and B are the same distance away	= **A et B sont aussi loin l'un que l'autre**
A is three kilometres nearer than B	= **A est plus près de trois kilomètres que B**

B is three kilometres further than A	= **B est plus loin de trois kilomètres que A**
the house is three kilometres too far	= **la maison est trop loin de trois kilomètres**
the plant is three kilometres too near	= **l'usine est trop près de trois kilomètres**

Width and breadth

Note that in the following examples, *broad* can be used instead of *wide*, and *breadth* instead of *width*.

QUESTIONS

what is the width of the river?	= **de quelle largeur est la rivière?** *or* **quelle est la largeur de la rivière?**

For the use of **de**, see *The use of* de *in measurements*.

how wide is it?	= **combien fait-elle de large/de largeur?**

ANSWERS

it's ten metres wide	= **elle fait dix mètres (de large/de largeur)**
its width is ten metres	= **sa largeur est de dix mètres**

COMPARISONS

the Rhône is wider than the Saône	= **le Rhône est plus large que la Saône**
the Saône is narrower than the Rhône	= **la Saône est moins large que le Rhône** *or* **la Saône est plus étroite que le Rhône**
the Rhône is ten metres wider than the Saône	= **le Rhône est plus large que la Saône de dix mètres**
the Saône is ten metres narrower than the Rhône	= **la Saône est plus étroite que le Rhône de dix mètres**
C is as wide as D	= **C est aussi large que D**
C is the same width as D	= **C a la même largeur que D** *or* **C est de la même largeur que D**

the two rivers are the same width	= **les deux rivières ont la même largeur** or **les deux rivières font la même largeur** or **les deux rivières sont de la même largeur**
it's three metres too wide	= **il est trop large de trois mètres** or **il fait trois mètres de trop**
it's three metres too narrow	= **il est trop étroit de trois mètres** or **il lui manque trois mètres en largeur**

OTHER PHRASES

a river fifty metres wide	= **une rivière de cinquante mètres de large/de largeur**
a ditch two metres wide	= **un fossé de deux mètres de large/de largeur**
a piece of cloth two metres in width	= **une pièce de tissu de deux mètres de large/de largeur**

Depth

QUESTIONS

what is the depth of the river?	= **quelle est la profondeur de la rivière?**
how deep is it?	= **combien fait-elle de profondeur?**

For the use of **de**, see *The use of* de *in measurements*.

ANSWERS

it's ten metres deep	= **elle fait dix mètres (de profondeur)**
its depth is ten metres	= **sa profondeur est de dix mètres**

COMPARISONS

A is deeper than B	= **A est plus profond que B**
B is shallower than A	= **B est moins profond que A**

(Note that French does not have an adjective corresponding to *shallow*.)

A is three metres deeper than B	= **A est plus profond que B de trois mètres**

C is as deep as D	=	**C est aussi profond que D**
C is the same depth as D	=	**C a la même profondeur que D**
the two tanks are the same depth	=	**les deux réservoirs ont la même profondeur** or **les deux réservoirs font la même profondeur**
it's three metres too deep	=	**il est trop profond de trois mètres** or **il fait trois mètres de trop en profondeur**
it's three metres too shallow	=	**il n'est pas assez profond de trois mètres** or **il lui manque trois mètres de profondeur** or **il lui manque trois mètres en profondeur**

OTHER PHRASES

at a depth of three metres	=	**à une profondeur de trois mètres**
the wreck is at a depth of ninety-five metres	=	**l'épave repose par quatre-vingt-quinze mètres de profondeur**
a river ten metres deep	=	**une rivière de dix mètres de profondeur**

....

Surface area

Surface area measurements

Note that French has a comma where English has a decimal point.

1 sq in = **6,45 cm² (centimètres carrés)***	1 acre = **40,47 ares**
1 sq ft = **929,03 cm² = 0,4 ha (hectares)**	
1 sq yd = **0,84 m² (mètres carrés)**	1 sq ml = **2,59 km² (kilomètres carrés)**

*There are three ways of saying **6,45 cm²**, and other measurements like it: **six virgule quarante-cinq centimètres carrés,** or (less formally) **six centimètres carrés virgule quarante-cinq,** or **six centimètres carrés quarante-cinq.**

For how to say numbers in French, see *Numbers*.

QUESTIONS

what is the area of your garden?	= **quelle est la superficie de votre jardin?**
what's its area?	= **quelle est sa surface?**

Note that **surface** and **superficie** are almost always synonymous.

ANSWERS

it's 200 square metres	= **il mesure 200 mètres carrés** *or* **il fait 200 mètres carrés**
its surface area is 200 square metres	= **sa surface est de 200 mètres carrés**

For the use of **de**, see *The use of* de *in measurements*.

it's 20 metres by 10 metres	= **il mesure 20 mètres sur 10 mètres**

COMPARISONS

my garden is bigger than yours	= **mon jardin est plus grand que le tien**
your garden is smaller than mine	= **ton jardin est plus petit que le mien** *or* **ton jardin est moins grand que le mien**
C is the same area as D	= **C a la même superficie que D**
C and D are the same area	= **C et D ont la même superficie/surface** *or* **C et D font la même superficie/surface**
my garden is 10 square metres bigger than yours	= **mon jardin est plus grand que le tien de 10 mètres carrés**

OTHER PHRASES

there are 10,000 square centimetres in a square metre	= **il y a 10 000 centimètres carrés dans un mètre carré**

10,000 square centimetres make one square metre	=	**10 000 centimètres carrés font un mètre carré**
sold by the square metre	=	**vendu au mètre carré**
six hectares of ground	=	**six hectares de terrain**

See also *Currencies and money*.

....

Capacity

Capacity measurement

British liquid measurements

| 20 fl oz | = **0,57 l (litre)** | 1 qt | = **1,13 l * (litres)** |
| 1 pt | = **0,57 l** | 1 gal | = **4,54 l** |

*There are three ways of saying **1,13 l**, and other measurements like it: **un virgule treize litres**, *or (less formally)* **un litre virgule treize**, or **un litre treize**.

American liquid measurements

| 16 fl oz | = **0,47 l** | 1 qt | = **0,94 l** |
| 1 pt | = **0,47 l** | 1 gal | = **3,78 l** |

For how to say numbers in French, see *Numbers*.

QUESTIONS

| what does the tank hold? | = | **combien le réservoir contient-il?** |
| what is its capacity? | = | **quelle est sa contenance?** |

ANSWERS

| its capacity is 200 litres | = | **sa contenance est de 200 litres** *or* **il contient 200 litres** *or* **il fait 200 litres** |

For the use of **de**, see *The use of* de *in measurements*.

COMPARISONS

| the bottle holds more than the carafe | = | **la bouteille contient plus que la carafe** |
| the bottle has a greater capacity than the carafe | = | **la bouteille a une plus grande contenance que la carafe** |

the carafe holds less than the bottle	=	**la carafe contient moins que la bouteille**
the carafe has a smaller capacity than the bottle	=	**la carafe a une moins grande contenance que la bouteille**
A holds 10 litres more than B	=	**A contient 10 litres de plus que B**
C has the same capacity as D	=	**C a la même contenance que D**
the two containers have the same capacity	=	**les deux containers ont la même contenance** *or* **les deux containers font la même contenance**

OTHER PHRASES

Note that the French calculate the petrol consumption of vehicles in litres per 100 km:

my new car does 28 miles to the gallon	≈	**ma nouvelle voiture fait dix litres aux cent kilomètres** *or* **ma nouvelle voiture fait dix litres aux cent**
a 200-litre tank	=	**un réservoir de 200 litres**
a tank over 200 litres	=	**un réservoir de plus de 200 litres**
sold by the litre	=	**vendu au litre**
six litres of wine	=	**six litres de vin**

See also *Currencies and money*.

....

Weight

Weight measurement

Note that French has a comma where English has a decimal point.

1 oz = **28,35 g* (grammes)**
1 lb† = **453,60 g**
1 st = **6,35 kg (kilos)**

1 cwt = **50,73 kg**
1 ton = **1014,60 kg**

*There are three ways of saying **28,35 g,** and other
measurements like it: **vingt-huit virgule trente-cinq
grammes,** or (less formally) **vingt-huit grammes virgule
trente-cinq,** or **vingt-huit grammes trente-cinq.**

†English a pound is translated by **une livre** in French, but
note that the French **livre** is actually 500 grams (half a
kilo).

For how to say numbers in French, see *Numbers*.

People

QUESTIONS

what is his weight? *or* how much does he weigh?	= **combien pèse-t-il?**

ANSWERS

he weighs 10 stone	≈ **il pèse 63 kilos 500** (*say* **soixante-trois kilos cinq cents**)
he weighs more than 20 stone	≈ **il pèse plus de 127 kilos**

COMPARISONS

Annette is heavier than Brigitte	= **Annette est plus lourde que Brigitte**
Brigitte is lighter than Annette	= **Brigitte est plus légère qu'Annette** *or* **Brigitte est moins lourde qu'Annette**

For the use of **de**, see *The use of* de *in measurements*.

Annette is 2 kilos heavier than Brigitte	= **Annette est plus lourde que Brigitte de 2 kilos**
Chris is as heavy as Deirdre	= **Chris est aussi lourd que Deirdre**

Chris is the same weight as Deirdre	= **Chris a le même poids que Deirdre** or **Chris fait le même poids que Deirdre**
Chris and Deirdre are the same weight	= **Chris et Deirdre ont le même poids** or **Chris et Deirdre font le même poids**
he is four pounds too heavy	≈ **il pèse deux kilos de trop** or **il fait deux kilos de trop**
he is four pounds too light	≈ **il lui manque deux kilos**

OTHER PHRASES

a 20-stone boxer	≈ **un boxeur de 120 kilos**
one thousand kilos make one ton	= **mille kilos font une tonne**

Things

QUESTIONS

what does the parcel weigh?	= **combien pèse le colis?**
how heavy is it?	= **quel poids fait-il?**

ANSWERS

it weighs ten kilos	= **il pèse dix kilos** or **il fait dix kilos**

COMPARISONS

the parcel is heavier than the letter	= **le colis est plus lourd que la lettre**
the parcel weighs more than the letter	= **le colis pèse plus que la lettre**
the letter is lighter than the parcel	= **la lettre est plus légère que le colis** or **la lettre est moins lourde que le colis**
the case is 2 kilos heavier than the book	= **la valise est plus lourde que le livre de 2 kilos**
C is as heavy as D	= **C est aussi lourd que D**

C is the same weight as D	= **C a le même poids que D** *or* **C fait le même poids que D**
the two books are the same weight	= **les deux livres ont le même poids** *or* **les deux livres font le même poids**
it is four pounds too heavy	= **il pèse 2 kilos de trop** *or* **il fait 2 kilos de trop**
it is four pounds too light	≈ **il est trop léger de 2 kilos** *or* **il lui manque 2 kilos**
it was 2 kilos overweight	≈ **il pesait deux kilos de trop**

OTHER PHRASES

sold by the kilo	= **vendu au kilo**
6 lbs of carrots	= **6 livres de carottes**
2 kilos of butter	= **2 kilos de beurre**
1.5 kilos of tomatoes	= **un kilo cinq cents de tomates**

See also *Currencies and money*.

there are about two pounds to a kilo	= **il y a environ deux livres dans un kilo**
a 3-lb potato	= **une pomme de terre de trois livres**
a parcel 3 kilos in weight	= **un colis de trois kilos**

....

Speed

Speed of road, rail, air etc. travel

In French, speed is measured in kilometres per hour:

100	kph	= **approximately 63 mph**
100	mph	= **approximately 160 kph**
50	mph	= **approximately 80 kph**

For how to say numbers in French, see *Numbers*.

35 miles per hour	= **35 miles à l'heure**
97 kilometres per hour	= **97 kilomètres à l'heure** *or* **97 kilomètres-heure** (*say* **quatre-vingt dix-sept kilomètres heure**)

QUESTIONS

what speed was the car going at?	=	**à quelle vitesse la voiture roulait-elle?**
how fast was the car going?	=	**à quelle vitesse roulait la voiture?**
what was the car doing?	=	**la voiture faisait du combien?** (*colloquial*)

ANSWERS

the speed of the car was 200 kph	=	**la vitesse de la voiture était de 200 km/h**

For the use of **de**, see *The use of* de *in measurements*.

it was going at 150 kph	=	**elle roulait à 150 km/h** (*say* à cent cinquante kilomètres-heure)
it was going at fifty (mph)	≈	**il/elle roulait à quatre-vingts à l'heure**
it was doing ninety (mph)	≈	**il/elle faisait du 150** (*colloquial*)
it was going at more than 200 kph	=	**il/elle roulait à plus de 200 km/h**
it was going at less than 40 kph	=	**il/elle roulait à moins de 40 km/h**

COMPARISONS

the car was going faster than the lorry	=	**la voiture roulait plus vite que le camion** *or* **la voiture allait plus vite que le camion**
the lorry was going slower than the car	=	**le camion roulait moins vite que la voiture** *or* **le camion allait moins vite que la voiture** *or* **le camion roulait plus lentement que la voiture** *or* **le camion allait plus lentement que la voiture**
A was going 10 kph faster than B	=	**A roulait à 10 km/h plus vite que B**
C was going at the same speed as D	=	**C roulait à la même vitesse que D** *or* **C allait à la même vitesse que D**

| the two vans were going at the same speed | = | **les deux camionnettes roulaient à la même vitesse** or **les deux camionnettes allaient à la même vitesse** |

OTHER PHRASES

| the speed of light is 186,300 miles per second | ≈ | **la vitesse de la lumière est de 300.000 km/s** (say **trois cent mille kilomètres par seconde** or **trois cent mille kilomètres à la seconde** or (colloquial) **trois cent mille kilomètres seconde**) |

| sound travels at 330 metres per second | = | **le son se déplace à 330 m/s** (say **à trois cent trente mètres par seconde** or (colloquial) **à trois cent mètres seconde**) |

Temperature

Temperatures in French are written as in the table below. Note the space in French between the figure and the degree sign and letter indicating the scale. When the scale letter is omitted, temperatures are written thus: 20°; 98,4° etc. (French has a comma, where English has a decimal point).

Note also that there is no capital on centigrade in French; capital C is however used as the abbreviation for **Celsius** and centigrade as in **60 °C**.

Celsius or centigrade (C)	Fahrenheit (F)	
100 °C	212 °F	**température d'ébullition de l'eau (boiling point)**
90 °C	194 °F	
80 °C	176 °F	
70 °C	158 °F	
60 °C	140 °F	
50 °C	122 °F	
40 °C	104 °F	

37 °C	**98,4 °F**	
30 °C	**86 °F**	
20 °C	**68 °F**	
10 °C	**50 °F**	
0 °C	**32 °F**	**température de congélation de l'eau (freezing point)**
–10 °C	**14 °F**	
–17,8 °C	**0 °F**	
–273,15 °C	**–459,67 °F**	**le zéro absolu (absolute zero)**

For how to say numbers in French, see *Numbers*.

People

QUESTIONS

what is his temperature? = **quelle est sa température?**

ANSWERS

his temperature is 40° = **il a quarante de température** (*or colloquial*) **il a quarante de fièvre**

For the use of **de**, see *The use of de in measurements*.

she is running a temperature of 39 = **elle a 39 de température**

Things

QUESTIONS AND ANSWERS

Note the obligatory use of **à** in the following:

what temperature is the milk? = **à quelle température est le lait?**

it is 40° C = **il est à 40° C** (*say* **il est à quarante degrés centigrade** *or* **il est à quarante degrés**)

what temperature does water boil at? = **à quelle température l'eau bout-elle?**

it boils at 100° C = **elle bout à 100° C** (*say* **elle bout à cent degrés centigrade** *or* **elle bout à cent degrés**)

at a temperature of 100° C = **à une température de 100° C**

COMPARISONS

A is hotter than B	= **A est plus chaud que B**
B is cooler than A	= **B est plus frais que A** *or* **B est moins chaud que A**
B is colder than A	= **B est plus froid que A** *or* **B est moins chaud que A**
A is 2° hotter than B	= **A est plus chaud que B de 2°**
C is the same temperature as D	= **C est à la même température que D**
C and D are the same temperature	= **C et D sont à la même température**

(Note that **à** is obligatory in the preceding constructions.)

Weather

QUESTIONS

what's the temperature today?	= **quelle température fait-il aujourd'hui?**
how cold/hot is it outside?	= **quelle température fait-il dehors?**

ANSWERS

it is 65° F	= **il fait 65° F** (*say* **il fait soixante-cinq degrés Fahrenheit**)
it is 40 degrees	= **il fait 40 degrés**
it is 40	= **il fait 40**

COMPARISONS

Lyon is warmer than Edinburgh	= **il fait plus chaud à Lyon qu'à Édimbourg**
Edinburgh is cooler than Lyon	= **il fait plus frais à Édimbourg qu'à Lyon**

| the temperature at A is 2° higher than at B | = **la température est plus haute à A qu'à B de 2°** |
| it is the same temperature in Paris as in London | = **il fait la même température à Paris qu'à Londres** |

....

Currencies and money

French money

write	say
25 c	**vingt-cinq centimes**
1 F*	**un franc**
1,50† F	**un franc cinquante** or **un franc cinquante centimes**
2 F	**deux francs**
2,75 F	**deux francs soixante-quinze**
20 F	**vingt francs**
100 F	**cent francs**
1 000 F	**mille francs**
1 000 000 F	**un million de francs‡**

*Note that French normally puts the abbreviation after the amount, unlike British (£1) or American ($1) English. However in some official documents amounts may be given as FF 2 000 000 etc.

†French uses a comma to separate units (e.g. 2,75 F), where English normally has a decimal point (e.g. £5.50).

‡The franc was revalued in the 1960s, when 100 old francs became 1 new franc. However, French people who were accustomed to counting in old francs still sometimes use these when referring to very large sums (e.g. the price of houses or cars), so deux millions de francs might very well mean 20 000 new francs instead of 2 000 000 francs.

For how to say numbers in French, see *Numbers*.

QUESTIONS

| how much is it? | = **combien est-ce que cela/ça coûte?** (*or colloquial*) **combien ça coûte?** (*or colloquial*) **c'est combien?** |
| how much is the book? | = **combien coûte le livre?** |

ANSWERS

it is 15 francs	= **cela/ça/il/elle coûte 15 francs**
the price is 15 francs	= **le prix est de 15 francs**

For the use of **de**, see *The use of* de *in measurements*.

the book costs 150 francs	= **le livre coûte 150 francs**
it costs over 150 francs	= **il coûte plus de 150 francs**
it costs just under 150 francs	= **il coûte un peu moins de 150 francs**

COMPARISONS

the house is more expensive than the flat	= **la maison est plus chère que l'appartement**
the flat is less expensive than the house	= **l'appartement est moins cher que la maison** (*or colloquial*) **l'appartement est meilleur marché que la maison**
A costs 2 francs more than B	= **A coûte plus cher que B de 2 francs**
the two computers are the same price	= **les deux ordinateurs font le même prix** *or* **les deux ordinateurs sont au même prix**

OTHER PHRASES

there are 6 francs to the dollar	= **le dollar vaut 6 francs**

Note the use of French **le** for English *a* in the following:

it costs 100 francs a metre	= **cela/ça coûte 100 francs le mètre** *or* **le mètre coûte 100 francs** (*or colloquial*) **le mètre fait 100 francs**

Similarly, **100 francs le mètre carré, 100 francs le litre, 100 francs le kilo**, etc.

The value of things

French uses **de** in the following:

a 100-franc note	= **un billet de cent francs**

a 5-franc coin	= **une pièce de cinq francs**
a £500 cheque	= **un chèque de cinq cent livres**
a two-thousand-pound grant	= **une bourse de deux mille livres**
a 100,000-pound house	= **une maison de 100 000 livres**
a 2 million-dollar deficit	= **un déficit de 2 millions de dollars**

But **en** is used in:

| a dollar check | = **un chèque en dollars** |
| a sterling traveller's cheque | = **un chèque de voyage en livres** |

And **à** is used in:

| a three-franc stamp | = **un timbre à trois francs** |
| a £10 ticket | = **un billet à dix livres** |

....

Sizes

In the following tables of equivalent sizes, French sizes have been rounded up, where necessary. (It is always better to have clothes a little too big than a little too tight.)

Men's shoe sizes		Women's shoe sizes		
in UK & US	in France	in UK	in US	in France
6	39	3	6	35
7	40	3½	6½	36
8	42	4	7	37
9	43	5	7½	38
10	44	6	8	39
11	45	7	8½	40
12	46	8	9	41

Men's clothing sizes		**Women's clothing sizes**		
in UK & US	in France	in UK	in US	in France
28	38	8	4	34
30	40	10	6	36
32	42	12	8	38–40
34	44	14	10	42
36	46	16	12	44–46
38	48	18	14	48
40	50	20	16	50
42	52			
44	54			
46	56			

Men's shirt collar sizes

in UK & US	in France	in UK & US	in France
14	36	16½	41
14½	37	17	42
15	38	17½	43
15½	39	18	44
16	40		

Note that for shoe and sock sizes French uses pointure, *so a size 37 is* une pointure 37. *For all other types of garment (even stockings and tights) the word* taille *is used, so a size 16 shirt is* une chemise taille 40, *etc.*

For how to say numbers in French, see *Numbers*.

QUESTIONS AND ANSWERS

what is your size?	= **quelle est votre taille?** *or* **quelle taille faites-vous?**
I take size 54	= **je fais du 54** *or* **je prends du 54** *or* **je porte du 54**
my shoe size is 43	= **je fais du 43** *or* **je prends du 43** *or* **je chausse du 43**
a pair of shoes size 43	= **une paire de chaussures pointure 43**
have you got the same thing in a 16?	≈ **avez-vous ce modèle en 40?**

have you got this in a smaller size?	=	**avez-vous ce modèle dans une plus petite taille?** *or* **avez-vous ce modèle en plus petit?**
have you got this in a larger size?	=	**avez-vous ce modèle dans une plus grande taille?** *or* **avez-vous ce modèle en plus grand?**
Annabel takes a size bigger than Bernard	=	**Annabel prend une taille plus grande que Bernard**
Chantal and Denise take the same shoe size	=	**Chantal et Denise ont la même pointure** *or* **Chantal et Denise font la même pointure**

Marks and grades

The French marking system

The French system tends to use a mark out of twenty. Letter grades are rare.

Note *out of* = **sur**:

| I got five out of ten | = | **j'ai eu cinq sur dix** |

The French scale has several key points:

dix sur vingt	=	**passable**
douze sur vingt	=	**assez bien**
quatorze sur vingt	=	**bien**
seize sur vingt	=	**très bien**

Sometimes English precedes the mark or grade with the indefinite article; French does not:

I got five/a five	≈	**j'ai eu dix**
this piece is only worth a three	≈	**ce travail ne mérite pas plus de six**
she got B/a B	≈	**elle a eu quatorze/'bien'**
he's hoping for a C	≈	**il espère avoir au moins douze/'assez bien'**

French only very rarely translates *mark* or *grade*:

it was awarded Grade B	≈ on a mis quinze à ce travail
I got a B grade	≈ j'ai eu quatorze (sur vingt)
I passed at Grade C	≈ j'ai été reçu avec douze (sur vingt)
I was hoping for a mark of eight	≈ j'espérais avoir seize

Weighting

Rather than marking out of more than twenty (e.g. 100) or out of less (e.g. 10), the French use a system of weighting via **coefficients**:

| the first two tests are double-weighted | = les deux premières épreuves ont le coefficient deux |

Notions like *pass* and *fail* preceded by adjectives are often translated by **note**:

a good pass	= une bonne note
a high pass	= une très bonne note
a narrow pass	= une note tout juste passable
a narrow fail	= une note presque suffisante
a bad fail	= une mauvaise note
a low fail	= une très mauvaise note

Note also

| a mark of 7 out of 10 | ≈ une note de 14 sur 20. |

Age

To be X years old

Note the use of **avoir** to translate English *be*:

how old is he?	= quel âge a-t-il?
what age are you?	= quel âge avez-vous?
I am forty years old	= j'ai quarante ans
she will soon be thirty years old	= elle aura bientôt trente ans

This construction is also used for objects:

the house is a hundred years old	=	**la maison a cent ans**

English can omit *years old* but in French **ans** cannot be omitted whatever the verb:

he is not yet sixty	=	**il n'a pas encore soixante ans**
she's just ten	=	**elle a tout juste dix ans**
he's barely twelve	=	**il a à peine douze ans**
I still feel sixteen	=	**j'ai toujours l'impression d'avoir seize ans**
he looks barely sixteen	=	**on lui donnerait à peine seize ans**

A person of X/aged X

a man of fifty	=	**un homme de cinquante ans** *or* **un homme âgé de cinquante ans**
a child of eight and a half	=	**un enfant de huit ans et demi** *or* **un enfant âgé de huit ans et demi**

Once again, **ans** must never be omitted.

âgé and **à l'âge** are followed by **de**:

a man aged thirty	=	**un homme (âgé) de trente ans**
a woman of fifty	=	**une femme (âgée) de cinquante ans**
at the age of forty	=	**à l'âge de quarante ans**

For the use of **de**, see *The use of* de *in measurements*.

An X-year-old person

A construction with **de** is also used in French for *an X-year-old person*:

they have a ten-year-old daughter	=	**ils ont une fille de dix ans**
an eighty-year-old pensioner	=	**un retraité de quatre-vingts ans**

| there aren't many fifty-year-old footballers | = des footballeurs de cinquante ans, il n'y en a pas beaucoup |

Expressions like *eight-year-old* used as nouns require a translation with a noun (or an expression like **quelqu'un**) in French:

they've got a ten-year-old and an eight-year-old	= ils ont un enfant de dix ans et un autre de huit ans
a sixty-year-old would never say that	= quelqu'un de soixante ans ne dirait jamais ça
Grandad's as sprightly as a thirty-year-old	= grand-père est aussi actif qu'un homme de trente ans

Approximate ages

There are a number of ways of giving approximate ages in French. One is to use a word ending in **-aine**:

| she's around forty | = elle a la quarantaine |
| he is about fifty | = il a une cinquantaine d'années |

(Note the use of **années** after words in **-aine** which are followed by **de**; **ans** is impossible here.)

Another is to use **environ**:

| they're both about thirty | = ils ont tous deux environ trente ans |

dans les is used colloquially:

| she must be around seventy | = elle doit avoir dans les soixante-dix ans |

Various translations are possible for English words ending in *-ties*:

| she's in her sixties | = elle a plus de soixante ans *or* elle a soixante ans passés *or* elle a entre soixante et soixante-dix ans |
| she's in her early sixties | = elle a entre soixante et soixante-cinq ans *or* elle a à peine soixante ans |

she's in her late sixties	≐	**elle va avoir soixante-dix ans** *or* (*more colloquial*) **elle va sur ses soixante-dix ans**
he's in his mid forties	=	**il a entre quarante et cinquante ans** *or* **il a environ quarante-cinq ans** *or* (*more colloquial*) **il a dans les quarante-cinq ans**

French words ending in **-énaire** are more numerous than English words ending in **-enarian**. Here is the complete list:

someone of forty	=	**un/une quadragénaire**
someone of fifty	=	**un/une quinquagénaire**
a person of sixty	=	**un/une sexagénaire**
a septuagenarian	=	**un/une septuagénaire**
an octogenarian	=	**un/une octogénaire**
a person of ninety	=	**un/une nonagénaire**

For *someone of a hundred* one can say:

un/une centenaire

All these French expressions can also be used as adjectives:

they are seventy/in their seventies	=	**ils sont septuagénaires**

over/under

Note once again that **ans** cannot be omitted:

she's just over sixty	=	**elle vient d'avoir soixante ans**
she's just under seventy	=	**elle aura bientôt soixante-dix ans**
he's just ten	=	**il a tout juste dix ans**
he's barely twelve	=	**il a à peine douze ans**
the under twelves	=	**les moins de douze ans**
the over eighties	=	**les plus de quatre-vingts ans**

older/younger

- Use **que** + person:

I'm older than you	= **je suis plus âgé que toi**
she's younger than Paul	= **elle est plus jeune que Paul**

- Use **de** to specify the age gap:

Anne is two years younger	= **Anne a deux ans de moins** *or* **Anne est plus jeune de deux ans**
Margot is five years older than Suzanne *or* Margot is older than Suzanne by five years	= **Margot a cinq ans de plus que Suzanne** *or* **Margot est plus âgée que Suzanne de cinq ans**
Robert is six years younger than Thomas *or* Robert is younger than Thomas by six years	= **Robert a six ans de moins que Thomas** *or* **Robert est plus jeune que Thomas de six ans**

Elements and materials

Chemicals

Here are the names of some common chemical elements. Note that the following are all masculine.

calcium	=	**calcium** *m*
carbon	=	**carbone** *m*
chlorine	=	**chlore** *m*
copper	=	**cuivre** *m*
hydrogen	=	**hydrogène** *m*
iron	=	**fer** *m*
magnesium	=	**magnésium** *m*
nitrogen	=	**azote** *m*
oxygen	=	**oxygène** *m*
sodium	=	**sodium** *m*
sulphur	=	**soufre** *m*
zinc	=	**zinc** *m*

As with other substances the names of chemicals normally take an article in French where English has none:

to study calcium	=	**étudier le calcium**
the properties of oxygen	=	**les propriétés de l'oxygène**
bauxite mining	=	**l'exploitation minière de la bauxite**
the production of magnesium	=	**la production du magnésium**

If the reference is to *a certain quantity of*, French uses **du**, **de l'**, or **de la**:

to produce oxygen	=	**produire de l'oxygène**
to add carbon	=	**ajouter du carbone**

Where English uses compound expressions, French normally uses two terms linked by de:

sodium chloride	=	**chlorure** *m* **de sodium**
sodium sulphate	=	**sulfate** *m* **de soude**
carbon monoxide	=	**oxyde** *m* **de carbone**
carbohydrate	=	**hydrate** *m* **de carbone**

Also:

carbon fibre	=	**fibre** *f* **de carbone**

but:

hydrogen peroxide	=	**eau oxygénée**
sulphur dioxide	=	**anhydride sulphureux**

Where English has *of* French has the equivalent de:

chloride of lime	=	**chlorure de chaux**

There are also compounds where the idea is *x works with a chemical*; here à is the commonest means of construction:

a hydrogen bomb	=	**une bombe à hydrogène**
a neon light	=	**une lampe au néon**

See also *Metals*.

....

Metals

Here are the names of some common metals. Note that the following are all masculine.

aluminium	=	**aluminium** *m*
bronze	=	**bronze** *m*
calcium	=	**calcium** *m*
chromium	=	**chrome** *m*
copper	=	**cuivre** *m*
gold	=	**or** *m*

iron	=	**fer** *m*
lead	=	**plomb** *m*
magnesium	=	**magnésium** *m*
platinum	=	**platine** *m*
potassium	=	**potassium** *m*
silver	=	**argent** *m*
sodium	=	**sodium** *m*
steel	=	**acier** *m*
tin	=	**étain** *m*
zinc	=	**zinc** *m*

As with other substances, the names of metals normally take an article in French where English has none:

to use copper	=	**utiliser le cuivre**
to mine gold	=	**extraire l'or**
the uses of lead	=	**les emplois du plomb**
the properties of zinc	=	**les propriétés du zinc**

If the reference is to *a certain quantity of*, French uses **du**, **de l'**, or **de la**:

| to produce silver | = | **produire de l'argent** |
| to add copper | = | **ajouter du cuivre** |

de and *en*

One of the main translation problems involves deciding when to use **de** and when **en**, whether translating English *of* or compounds like *tin cup*. The following remarks are guidelines rather than rules.

When words for metals are used (like adjectives) as the first element in compounds, both **en** and **de** are found:

With **en** preferred (but **de** is not impossible):

| bronze jewellery | = | **des bijoux en bronze** |

a tin cup	=	**une tasse en étain**
an aluminium plate	=	**un plat en aluminium**
a bronze coin	=	**une pièce en bronze**
silver cutlery	=	**des couverts en argent**

With **de** preferred (but **en** is not impossible):

an iron bar	=	**une barre de fer**
a gold ingot	=	**un lingot d'or**
a lead pipe	=	**un tuyau de plomb**
silver wire	=	**du fil d'argent**
a platinum disc	=	**un disque de platine**
aluminium ore	=	**du minerai d'aluminium**
a cadmium deposit	=	**un dépôt de cadmium**
gold coins	=	**des pièces d'or**

When translating *with* use **de**, not **en**:

| lined with zinc | = | **doublé de zinc** |
| covered with silver | = | **recouvert d'argent** |

but note:

| gold-plated | = | **plaqué or** |
| silver-plated | = | **plaqué argent** |

Obviously, when the meaning is not *made of*, French uses **de**, and **en** is impossible:

zinc alloy	=	**un alliage de zinc**
an iron mine	=	**une mine de fer**
a gold prospector	=	**un chercheur d'or**

Distinguish:

| a gold medal | = | **une médaille en or** (*i.e. made of gold*) *vs.* **une médaille d'or** (*i.e. the winner's medal*) |

Note also cases like:

a steel refinery	=	**une aciérie**

For figurative expressions, **de** is more usual:

a heart of gold	=	**un cœur d'or**
an iron fist in a velvet glove	=	**une main de fer dans un gant de velours**
muscles of steel	=	**des muscles d'acier**

but:

a golden chance	=	**une occasion en or**

For *gold, silver, bronze* (= medals), see also *Sport*.

....

Manufacturing materials

Here are the names of some common manufacturing materials.

Building materials

brick	=	**brique** *f*
cast iron	=	**fonte** *f*
concrete	=	**béton** *m*
glass	=	**verre** *m*
iron	=	**fer** *m*
steel	=	**acier** *m*
stone	=	**pierre** *f*
wood	=	**bois** *m*

Other materials

cardboard	=	**carton** *m*
china	=	**porcelaine** *f*
paper	=	**papier** *m*

plastic	= **plastique** *m*
pottery	= **faïence** *f*
rubber	= **caoutchouc** *m*
terra cotta	= **terre** *f* **cuite**

See also *Metals*.

As with other substances, the names of manufacturing materials normally take an article in French where English has none:

brick production	= **la production de la brique**
steel processing	= **le travail de l'acier**
plastic production	= **la production de** *or* **du plastique**

If the reference is to *a certain quantity of*, French uses **du, de l'**, *or* **de la**:

| to produce china | = **produire de la porcelaine** |
| to add rubber | = **ajouter du caoutchouc** |

de and *en*

One of the main translation problems involves deciding when to use **de** and when **en**, whether translating English *of* or compounds like *brick wall*. The following remarks are guidelines rather than rules.

When words for manufacturing materials are used (like adjectives) as the first element in compounds, both **en** and **de** are found:

With **en** preferred (but **de** is not impossible):

a concrete building	= **un bâtiment en béton**
a concrete road surface	= **une chaussée en ciment**
a plastic box	= **une boîte en plastique**
a plastic bag	= **un sac en plastique**

With **de** preferred (but **en** is not impossible):

| a steel slab | = **une plaque d'acier** |
| a brick path | = **une allée de briques** |

a concrete block	= **un bloc de béton**
a glass sheet	= **une plaque de verre**
brick coating	= **un doublage de briques**
a steel column	= **une colonne d'acier**
a glass eye	= **un œil de verre**
a wooden bridge	= **un pont de bois**
a thatch roof	= **un toit de chaume**

After the words **fabriqué** or **construit**, use **en**, not **de**:

a building made of steel	= **un bâtiment construit en acier**
a bridge made of wood	= **un pont construit en bois**
toys made with plastic	= **des jouets fabriqués en plastique**

But after **couvert**, use **de**, not **en**:

a thatch(ed) roof	= **un toit couvert de chaume**

....

Fabrics and textiles

Here are the names of some common fabrics and textiles.

acetate	= **acétate** *m*
cotton	= **coton** *m*
fur	= **fourrure** *f*
leather	= **cuir** *m*
linen	= **lin** *m*
nylon	= **nylon** *m*
polyester	= **polyester** *m*
silk	= **soie** *f*
vinyl	= **vinyle** *m*
viscose	= **viscose** *f*
wool	= **laine** *f*

As with other substances, the names of fabrics and
textiles normally take an article in French where
English has none:

silk is a natural fibre	=	**la soie est une fibre naturelle**
I can't wear wool next to my skin	=	**je ne peux pas porter de la laine à même la peau**

Some English expressions use the plural. French normally prefers the singular, keeping the plural to express special meanings:

dressed in silks	=	**habillée de soie** (**de soieries** would mean *with different types of extremely expensive fabrics*)
they were dressed in furs	=	**ils portaient de la fourrure** (**des fourrures** would mean *dressed in nondescript pieces of fur*)

If the reference is to *a certain quantity of*, French uses **du**, **de l'**, or **de la**:

to produce leather	=	**produire du cuir**
to add silk	=	**ajouter de la soie**

Compare with expressions where the reference is not to the quantity, but to the nature of the material:

to work leather	=	**travailler le cuir**

de and en

One of the main translation problems involves deciding when to use **de** and when **en**, whether translating English *of* or compounds like *silk shirt*. The following remarks are guidelines rather than rules.

When words for manufacturing materials are used (like adjectives) as the first element in compounds, both **en** and **de** are found:

en seems to be preferred when referring to materials that are not *noble*. In the following, **de** is not impossible:

a polyester-cotton sheet	=	**un drap en polyester et coton**
a vinyl handbag	=	**un sac à main en vinyle**

de is preferred when referring to *noble* materials. In the following, **en** is not impossible:

silk stockings	= **des bas de soie**
a linen curtain	= **un rideau de lin**

There are many cases where both seem equally acceptable:

a cotton towel	= **une serviette de** *or* **en coton**
leather gloves	= **des gants de** *or* **en cuir**
an acetate lining	= **une doublure d'acétate** *or* **en acétate**
a fur hat	= **un chapeau de** *or* **en fourrure**
velvet ribbon	= **du ruban de** *or* **en velours**
a wool carpet	= **un tapis de** *or* **en laine**
woollen socks	= **des chaussettes de** *or* **en laine**

However,

en is impossible when the expression refers to the textile itself in its various forms rather than to something that is made with that textile:

nylon filament	= **du filament de nylon**
nylon net	= **du voile de nylon**
silk thread	= **du fil de soie**
wool fibres	= **des fibres de laine**
wool yarn	= **du fil de laine**

or in the following, where English has *of*:

a reel of cotton	= **une bobine de coton**
a ball of wool	= **une pelote de laine**
a metre of silk	= **un mètre de soie**
a bale of cotton	= **une balle de coton**

Where places or processes are referred to, only **de** is possible, often with the definite article:

silk weaving	=	**le tissage de la soie**
cotton spinning	=	**la filature du coton**
a cotton mill	=	**une filature de coton**

Precious stones

Here are the names of some common precious and semi-precious stones.

Masculine names:

amber	=	**ambre**
coral	=	**corail**
diamond	=	**diamant**
garnet	=	**grenat**
jade	=	**jade**
jasper	=	**jaspe**
jet	=	**jais**
lapis lazuli	=	**lapis-lazuli**
ruby	=	**rubis**
sapphire	=	**saphir**

Feminine names:

agate	=	**agate**
amethyst	=	**améthyste**
aquamarine	=	**aigue-marine**
emerald	=	**émeraude**
malachite	=	**malachite**
moonstone	=	**pierre de lune**
mother of pearl	=	**nacre**
opal	=	**opale**
topaz	=	**topaze**
turquoise	=	**turquoise**

As with other substances, the names of stones normally
take an article in French where English has none. Note
that French sometimes prefers the singular:

I can't wear sapphires	=	**le saphir ne me va pas**
more precious than rubies	=	**plus précieux que le rubis**

If the reference is to *a certain quantity of* French uses **du,
de l'**, or **de la**:

to import jet	=	**importer du jais**
to use mother-of-pearl	=	**utiliser de la nacre**
to mine diamonds	=	**extraire des diamants**

de and *en*

One of the main translation problems involves deciding
when to use **de** and when **en**, whether translating
English *of* or compounds like *emerald ring*. In general,
only **de** is possible where the piece of jewellery uses
precious stones as an ornament, but is not entirely made
of that stone (note the use of the plural):

a diamond necklace	=	**une rivière de diamants**
a pearl necklace	=	**un collier de perles**

Compare:

a gold bracelet	=	**un bracelet en or** (*where the bracelet is entirely made of gold*)

Note also:

a diamond mine	=	**une mine de diamants**

but:

a diamond merchant	=	**un diamantaire**

In some cases, **avec** is preferable for clarity:

an emerald ring	=	**une bague avec une émeraude** *or* **avec des émeraudes**

| sapphire earrings | = **des boucles d'oreilles avec un saphir** or **avec des saphirs** |

For precious metals such as gold and silver see also *Metals*.

....

Colours

Here are some common colours:

black	= **noir/-e**
blue	= **bleu/-e**
green	= **vert/-e**
grey	= **gris/-e**
red	= **rouge**
white	= **blanc/blanche**
yellow	= **jaune**

Use of articles with colour nouns

The definite article is used in the following cases. Note that in French the names of colours are always masculine:

I like green	= **j'aime le vert**
she prefers yellow	= **elle préfère le jaune**
red suits you	= **le rouge vous va bien**

The indefinite article works best in the following examples where the colour term is further qualified:

| it's a pretty pink | = **c'est un joli rose** |
| it was a dreadful green | = **c'était un vert affreux** |

Occasionally, the partitive article is used:

| to wear white | = **porter du blanc** |

Agreement of colour adjectives

Normally colour adjectives agree in the usual way:

a blue dress	=	**une robe bleue**
black clothes	=	**des vêtements noirs**

But note these cases where there is no agreement, either in the feminine or in the plural:

Where the French word is really a noun:

a brown shoe	=	**une chaussure marron**
orange carpets	=	**des tapis orange**
hazel eyes	=	**les yeux noisette**

Colours named after flowers (e.g. **jonquille, lilas**) also belong to this category, with the exception of **rose** and **violet/violette**, which do agree.

However, the following are also invariable:

cherry-red	=	**cerise**
chocolate-brown	=	**chocolat**
emerald-green	=	**émeraude**

and other gem colours: **rubis**, etc.

Where colour terms are compound:

● Pale; dark, etc.

a pale blue shirt	=	**une chemise bleu pâle**
dark green blankets	=	**des couvertures vert foncé**
a light yellow tie	=	**une cravate jaune clair**
bright yellow socks	=	**des chaussettes jaune vif**

With such expressions it is possible to add **d'un** (this is especially common with the comparative or the superlative):

he had deep blue eyes	=	**il avait les yeux d'un bleu profond**
the dress was a darker blue	=	**la robe était d'un bleu plus foncé**

- Navy-blue, etc. (i.e. compound expressions where the colour term is qualified by a noun):

a navy-blue jacket	=	**une veste bleu marine**
sky-blue ribbons	=	**des rubans bleu ciel**
an apple-green dress	=	**une robe vert pomme**
peony-red dresses	=	**des robes rose pivoine**

Similarly:

midnight blue	=	**bleu nuit**
blood red	=	**rouge sang**

- Blue-black, etc. (i.e. terms consisting of two colour expressions, hyphenated):

a blue-black material	=	**une étoffe bleu-noir**
a greenish-blue cup	=	**une tasse bleu-vert**
greeny-yellow hats	=	**des chapeaux vert-jaune**

Colouring things

en is usual in the following constructions:

to paint a wall green	=	**peindre un mur en vert**
to dye one's hair red	=	**teindre ses cheveux en rouge**
to stain a door (in) light oak	=	**teindre une porte en chêne clair**

Also:

have you got this in white?	=	**est-ce que vous l'avez en blanc?**

Dressing in colours

de is used in the following:

to be dressed in black	=	**être habillé de noir**
a pretty shade of blue	=	**un joli ton de bleu**
a range of greens	=	**une gamme de verts**

For English expressions ending in -*coloured*, French uses
couleur + colour term:

rose-coloured fabrics	=	**des étoffes couleur rose**
flesh-coloured tights	=	**un collant couleur chair**

-ish

When translating English colour terms ending in -*ish*
note that the French words ending in -**âtre** are generally
rather negative in tone:

a blueish tinge	=	**un teint bleuâtre**
a greyish dress	=	**une robe grisâtre**

To avoid any problems here, it is safer to use **tirant sur le**:

a nice reddish brown	=	**une beau brun tirant sur le rouge**

blacken, etc.

French has a number of verbs ending in -**ir** equivalent to
English verbs ending in -*en*:

to blacken	=	**noircir**
to whiten	=	**blanchir**

Also: **bleuir, jaunir, rosir, rougir, verdir**.

But it is always safe to use **devenir**:

to go purple	=	**devenir violet**

Flora and fauna

Animals

Lists of animals

Here are the names of some common animals:

Domestic animals

cat	=	**chat** *m*/**chatte** *f*
dog	=	**chien** *m*/**chienne** *f*
guinea-pig	=	**cochon** *m* **d'Inde** *or* **cobaye** *m*
hamster	=	**hamster** *m*
rabbit	=	**lapin** *m*/**lapine** *f*

Farmyard animals

ox	=	**bœuf** *m* (*plural* **bœufs** - *pronounced* beu *as in* **deux**)
cow	=	**vache** *f*
donkey	=	**âne** *m* (*female donkey/jenny* = **ânesse** *f*)
goat	=	**chèvre** *f*
horse	=	**cheval** *m*
pig	=	**cochon** *m* *or* **porc** *m*
sheep	=	**mouton** *m*

Wild (including hunted) animals

badger	=	**blaireau** *m*
bear	=	**ours** *m*/**ourse** *f*
boar	=	**sanglier** *m*
cheetah	=	**guépard** *m*
deer	=	**cerf** *m*
fallow deer	=	**daim** *m*
roe deer	=	**chevreuil** *m*
elephant	=	**éléphant** *m*

fox	= **renard** *m*
hare	= **lièvre** *m*
leopard	= **léopard** *m*
lion	= **lion** *m*
skunk	= **mouffette** *f*
tiger	= **tigre** *m*
wolf	= **loup** *m*

Male, female, and young

Both English and French have groups of words to refer to adult male, adult female and young of certain species.

Masculine/feminine forms

French has two possibilities for showing sex differences between animals.

Either there are separate forms for male and female animals, or the forms are similar and the feminine form is derived from the masculine by addition of an ending.

Forms for young animals

In most cases where there is a separate term in French, this has a form related to one or both of the terms for the adult animal. Note from the lists that some words for young animals end in **-eau** and some in **-on** (both endings are always masculine). There are also forms quite distinct from those used to refer to the adult animals.

Distinct masculine and feminine forms (with terms for the young, where appropriate)

Note that these apply mainly to the larger and domestic animals:

bull/cow/calf	= **taureau** *m*/**vache** *f*/**veau** *m*
ram/ewe/lamb	= **bélier** *m*/**brebis** *f*/**agneau** *m*
boar/sow/piglet	= **verrat** *m*/**truie** *f*/**porcelet** *m*
stallion/mare/foal	= **étalon** *m*/**jument** *f*/**poulain** *m*

billy-goat/nanny goat/   = **bouc** *m*/**chèvre** *f*/**chevreau** *m*
  kid

Also:

he-monkey/she-monkey = **singe** *m*/**guenon** *f*

Related forms (with term for young where appropriate)

he-donkey/jenny/   = **âne** *m*/**ânesse** *f*/**ânon** *m*
  donkey foal

he-rat/she-rat/baby rat = **rat** *m*/**rate** *f*/**raton** *m*

he-cat/she-cat/kitten   = **chat** *m*/**chatte** *f*/**chaton** *m*

he-elephant/   = **éléphant** *m*/**éléphante** *f*/
  she-elephant/baby   **éléphanteau** *m*
  elephant

fox/vixen/fox cub   = **renard** *m*/**renarde** *f*/**renardeau** *m*

male lion/female lion/   = **lion** *m*/**lionne** *f*/**lionceau** *m*
  baby lion

buck rabbit/doe/baby   = **lapin** *m*/**lapine** *f*/**lapereau** *m*
  rabbit

he-wolf/she-wolf/wolf   = **loup** *m*/**louve** *f*/**louveteau** *m*
  cub

dog/bitch/puppy   = **chien** *m*/**chienne** *f*/**chiot** *m*

Also:

he-tiger/tigress   = **tigre** *m*/**tigresse** *f*

In cases where there is no accepted term, sex can be
shown in French by adding **mâle** or **femelle** after the word
for the species:

a male mouse   = **une souris mâle**

a she-cougar   = **un cougar femelle**

The species and individual animals; use of the article and of singular/plural

On the whole French uses the definite article in the same
way as English to refer to the species in general:

the cat is a domestic animal	= **le chat est un animal domestique**
the fiercest animal is the bear	= **l'ours est l'animal le plus féroce**
not forgetting the wild rabbit	= **sans oublier le lapin de garenne**

The definite article is also used when referring to a sub-species:

the African elephant	= **l'éléphant d'Afrique**
the milk cow	= **la vache laitière**

In speaking of the species using the plural, English has no article whereas French uses the definite article:

cats are bred for their looks	= **on élève les chats pour leur beauté**
bitches are sterilized on demand	= **les chiennes sont stérilisées sur demande**
an identity card for dogs	= **une carte d'identité pour les chiens**

Occasionally English plural forms, with or without plural -s, are translated by the singular with definite article in French to refer to the species:

to hunt lion	= **chasser le lion**

Speaking of one animal as a member of its species, both languages use the indefinite article:

if you have a dog, muzzle it	= **si vous avez un chien, muselez-le**
to keep a pet rabbit	= **avoir un lapin domestique**

and also in set phrases:

as cunning as a fox	= **rusé comme un renard**

Translating English compound expressions

English compounds are often translated by French expressions with **de**:

cow dung	= **de la bouse de vache**
a deer herd *or* a herd of deer	= **un troupeau de daims**
a lion hunter	= **un chasseur de lions**
a leopard skin	= **une peau de léopard**

French forms with **de** are also used as equivalents for English forms with *'s*:

| a lion's mane | = **une crinière de lion** |
| a tiger's lair | = **un antre de tigre** |

But in some cases the translation uses a different construction:

horse feed	= **de la nourriture pour chevaux**
dog behaviour	= **le comportement du chien**
mad cow disease	= **la maladie de la vache folle**

Use of *à* for hunting

This is used both for the prey...

bear hunting	= **la chasse à l'ours**
roe deer hunting	= **la chasse au chevreuil**
a boar hunt	= **une chasse au sanglier**

...and for the means of hunting:

| falconry | = **la chasse au faucon** |
| to hunt with bow and arrow | = **chasser à l'arc** |

See also *Food substances* for expressions concerning animals used for food (*veal, beef*, etc.).

....

Birds

Here are the names of some common birds. Note that there are more masculine than feminine names for birds, though both genders are common.

blackbird	= **merle** *m*
budgerigar	= **perruche** *f*
crow	= **corneille** *f or* **corbeau** *m* (**corbeau** is the generic term)
eagle	= **aigle** *m*
parrot	= **perroquet** *m*
partridge	= **perdrix** *f*
pheasant	= **faisan** *m*
robin	= **rouge-gorge** *m*
seagull	= **mouette** *f*
sparrow	= **moineau** *m*
starling	= **étourneau** *m or* **sansonnet** *m*
thrush	= **grive** *f*

For a few types of bird, mainly farmyard birds, there are separate masculine and feminine forms, and a form for the young:

drake/duck/duckling	= **canard** *m*/**cane** *f*/**caneton** *m*
gander/goose/gosling	= **jars** *m*/**oie** *f*/**oison** *m*
cock turkey/hen turkey/ baby turkey	= **dindon** *m*/**dinde** *f*/**dindonneau** *m*
cock/hen/chick	= **coq** *m*/**poule** *f*/**poussin** *m*

The species and individual birds; use of the article and of singular/plural

On the whole French uses the definite article in the same way as English to refer to the species in general:

the characteristics of the duck	= **les caractéristiques du canard**
the ancestors of the goose	= **les ancêtres de l'oie**
the condor is a species of vulture	= **le condor est une espèce de vautour**

The definite article can also be used when referring to a

sub-species:

the Andean condor	= **le condor des Andes**
the bald eagle	= **l'aigle chauve**

In speaking of the species using the plural, English has
no article whereas French uses the definite article:

chickens have a crop	= **les poules ont un jabot**
eagles have broad wings	= **les aigles ont de grandes ailes**
the breeding sites of gulls	= **les lieux de reproduction des mouettes**

Where English has no -*s*, French has the normal plural
form (but see below):

a flock of tern	= **une volée de sternes**
a flight of duck	= **un vol de canards**
a covey of partridge	= **un vol de perdrix**

Speaking of one bird as a typical member of its species,
both languages can use the indefinite article:

lots of old people keep a parrot	= **beaucoup de vieilles gens ont un perroquet**

Translating English compound expressions

The principal way of translating English compound
expressions into French is to use **de**:

goose feathers	= **des plumes d'oie**
a pigeon fancier	= **un amateur de pigeons**

French forms with **de** are also used as equivalents for
English forms in '*s*:

an eagle's nest	= **un nid d'aigle**
duck's eggs	= **des œufs de canard**
a cuckoo's nest	= **un nid de coucou**

But for shooting/hunting French uses constructions
with **à**, often with the plural:

duck shooting	=	**la chasse au canard** *or* **aux canards**
a pheasant shoot	=	**une chasse au faisan**
pigeon shooting	=	**la chasse à la palombe**

See also *Food substances* for expressions such as *chicken sandwich/wing/leg/breast*, etc.

....

Fish

Here are some common names of fish, and of certain sea mammals:

bream	=	**brème** *f*
carp	=	**carpe** *f*
cod	=	**morue** *f*
haddock	=	**aiglefin** *m* (smoked haddock = **du haddock**)
herring	=	**hareng** *m*
mackerel	=	**maquereau** *m*
mullet: grey mullet	=	**mulet** *m* (red mullet = **rouget** *m*)
perch	=	**perche** *f*
pike	=	**brochet** *m*
plaice	=	**carrelet** *m*
salmon	=	**saumon** *m*
trout	=	**truite** *f*
tuna	=	**thon** *m*
dolphin	=	**dauphin** *m*
porpoise	=	**marsouin** *m*
whale	=	**baleine** *f*
seal	=	**phoque** *m*
sealion	=	**lion** *m* **de mer**
walrus	=	**morse** *m*

For crustaceans, such as *crab, lobster*, etc. see *Food substances*.

The species and individual fish: use of the article and of singular/plural

On the whole French uses the definite article in the same way as English to refer to the species in general:

the habitat of the trout	=	**l'habitat de la truite**
the victims of the pike	=	**les victimes du brochet**
the carp and its predators	=	**la carpe et ses prédateurs**

The definite article is also used when referring to a sub-species:

the sea-trout	=	**la truite de mer**
the rainbow trout	=	**la truite arc-en-ciel**

In speaking of the species using the plural, English uses a form without -s and no article whereas French uses the definite article:

herring are no longer abundant	=	**les harengs ne sont plus très nombreux**
mullet are good to eat	=	**les rougets sont bons à manger**

In other cases where English uses a form without -s, French uses various forms:

you can see salmon in this stream	=	**il y a des saumons dans ce ruisseau**
to fish for trout	=	**pêcher la truite**
she caught several bream	=	**elle a pris plusieurs brêmes**

And there are also cases where English has the final -s but no article; French always uses an article:

you often see whales in the bay	=	**on voit souvent des baleines dans la baie**
breeding grounds for seals	=	**les lieux de reproduction des phoques**

Where English uses the indefinite article + singular to refer to typical members of a species, French prefers the definite article + singular:

| does a perch have scales? | = | **la perche a-t-elle des écailles?** |
| a trout seeks out shady areas | = | **la truite recherche les endroits ombragés** |

Translating English compound expressions

The principal way of translating English compound expressions into French is to use **de**:

a fish scale	=	**une écaille de poisson**
a trout farm	=	**un élevage de truites**
shark skin	=	**de la peau de requin**

This also applies to cases where English has forms with '*s*:

crab's claws	=	**des pinces de crabe**
shark's fins	=	**des ailerons de requin**
cod's eggs	=	**des œufs de cabillaud**

For names of types of fish, French sometimes has expressions using **de**...

| a farm trout | = | **une truite d'élevage** |
| a sea trout | = | **une truite de mer** |

...and sometimes (as seen above) an expression with the name of the fish + complement:

| a rainbow trout | = | **une truite arc-en-ciel** |
| a gilt-head bream | = | **une daurade royale** |

Note the use of **à** for objects with a purpose connected with fishing:

a salmon rod	=	**une canne à saumon**
a shrimp net	=	**un filet à crevettes**
a lobster pot	=	**un casier à homards**

and, with the definite article:

| harpooning | = | **la chasse au harpon** |

Note the following patterns:

chasse/pêche à + definite article + (name of fish)
chasser/pêcher + definite article + (name of fish)
chasseur/pêcheur de + (name of fish in plural)

whale hunting	= **la chasse à la baleine**
sardine fishing	= **la pêche à la sardine**
salmon fishing	= **la pêche au saumon**
to go tuna fishing	= **partir pêcher le thon** or **à la pêche au thon**
to like salmon fishing	= **aimer pêcher le saumon** or **la pêche au saumon**
they go whale hunting	= **il partent chasser la baleine** or **à la chasse à la baleine**
a trout fisherman	= **un pêcheur de truites**
a whale hunter	= **un chasseur de baleines**

See also *Food substances*.

Trees

Here are the names of some common trees. Note that in French they are all masculine:

ash	= **frêne** *m*
beech	= **hêtre** *m*
elm	= **orme** *m*
hazel (tree)	= **noisetier** *m*
oak	= **chêne** *m*
pine (tree)	= **pin** *m*
silver birch	= **bouleau** *m*
yew	= **if** *m*

and the following, used for furniture (see also *Materials*):

ebony	= **ébène** *m*
mahogany	= **acajou** *m*

| teak | = **te(c)k** *m* |
| walnut | = **noyer** *m* |

Fruit trees (also masculine) often end in **-ier**:

apple tree	= **pommier** *m*
lemon tree	= **citronnier** *m*
pear tree	= **poirier** *m*
(flowering) cherry (tree)	= **cerisier** *m*
wild cherry (tree)	= **merisier** *m*

but:

| orange tree | = **oranger** *m* |
| peach tree | = **pêcher** *m* |

Here are the names of some shrubs; most are masculine, but note the first items:

clematis	= **clématite** *f*
hawthorn	= **aubépine** *f*
wisteria	= **glycine** *f*
forsythia	= **forsythia** *m*
jasmine	= **jasmin** *m*
laburnum	= **cytise** *m*
lilac	= **lilas** *m*
rhododendron	= **rhododendron** *m*

The species and individual trees: use of the article and of singular/plural

On the whole French uses the definite article in the same way as English to refer to the species in general:

| the oak is a tree which... | = **le chêne est un arbre qui...** |
| the characteristics of the beech | = **les caractéristiques du hêtre** |

And, for such general expressions, both languages can choose between the singular and the plural (the plural in

French being preceded by the definite article):

the elm is a beautiful tree/elms are beautiful trees	= **l'orme est un bel arbre/les ormes sont de beaux arbres**

The definite article is also used when referring to a sub-species:

the use of the holm oak	= **l'utilisation du chêne vert**
the characteristics of the Scots pine	= **les caractéristiques du pin sylvestre**

In speaking of trees in general using the plural, English has no article whereas French uses an article:

why do they keep planting pines?	= **pourquoi continuent-ils à planter des pins?**
we would like to reintroduce elms	= **nous aimerions réintroduire des ormes**

The singular is also used:

to plant oaks	= **planter des chênes** or **du chêne**

In speaking of one tree, English often has a choice: we can speak of *an oak* or of *an oak tree*. French has no such choice and uses the simple word for the tree concerned:

to cut down an oak or an oak tree	= **abattre un chêne**
an old beech or beech tree	= **un vieux hêtre**

Both languages can use the indefinite article when speaking of a (= any) tree:

they often nest in an oak	= **ils font souvent leur nid dans un chêne**

In speaking of trees in general using the plural, English sometimes uses a form without -s and no article whereas French uses the usual plural form:

a forest of oak or oaks	= **une forêt de chênes**

Translating English compound expressions

As usual, French uses **de** in many cases, usually with the plural in collective expressions:

| an oak wood | = **un bois de chênes** |
| a pine forest | = **une forêt de pins** |

But the singular is more usual in expressions referring to parts of trees or items derived from trees:

an oak leaf	= **une feuille de chêne**
a pine cone	= **une pomme de pin**
beech bark	= **de l'écorce de hêtre**
a hazel twig	= **une brindille de noisetier**
a plane branch	= **une branche de platane**
an elm log	= **une bûche d'orme**

For furniture etc. made of wood, e.g. *pine furniture; an oak parquet floor*, see *Furniture*.

For expressions such as: *to dye furniture mahogany, to stain a chest walnut, a light oak wardrobe*, see *Colours*.

....

Flowers and perfumes

Flowers

Here are the names of some common flowers:

anemone	= **anémone** *f*
carnation	= **œillet** *m*
daisy	= (*wild*) **pâquerette** *f*; (*cultivated*) **marguerite** *f*
hyacinth	= **jacinthe** *f*
lily	= **lis** *m*
lily of the valley	= **muguet** *m*
pansy	= **pensée** *f*

primula, primrose	=	**primevère** f
rose	=	**rose** f
wild rose	=	**églantine** f
tulip	=	**tulipe** f
violet	=	**violette** f

As in English, the name of the flower in French is used to refer to the plant:

| to plant daisies | = | **planter des marguerites** |

French does, however, have separate words for the plants corresponding to **rose** and to **églantine** (= *wild rose*):

| the rose cannot be grown in such soil | = | **le rosier ne se cultive pas dans ce genre de sol** |
| the wild rose grew everywhere in the wood | = | **l'églantier poussait partout dans le bois** |

See also *Trees*.

The species and individual flowers: use of the article and of singular/plural

On the whole French uses the definite article in the same way as English to refer to the species in general:

| the anemone has been used in medicine | = | **l'anémone a été utilisée en médecine** |
| the wild rose grows easily here | = | **l'églantier pousse bien ici** |

In speaking of the species using the plural, English has no article whereas French uses the definite article:

| tulips cannot be grown in such soil | = | **les tulipes ne se cultivent pas dans ce genre de sol** |
| tulips are grown in Holland | = | **les tulipes sont cultivées aux Pays-Bas** |

Speaking of one flower as a member of its species, both languages can use the indefinite article:

| the best man should wear a carnation | = | **le garçon d'honneur devrait porter un œillet** |

des is used, as usual in French, when speaking of unspecified quantities. This is true both in general expressions...

| carnations are popular as button-holes | = | **on met souvent des œillets à la boutonnière** |

...and also when speaking of more specific groups of flowers:

| there are pansies in every bed | = | **il y a des pensées dans tous les parterres** |
| people were picking daffodils | = | **les gens cueillaient des jonquilles** |

Translating English compound expressions

English compounds are often translated by French expressions with **de**:

a daffodil bulb	=	**un bulbe de jonquille**
a lily petal	=	**un pétale de lis**
a rose bud	=	**un bouton de rose**
a rose bed	=	**un parterre de roses**
a rose border	=	**une bordure de roses**
rose water	=	**de l'eau de rose**

Perfumes, etc.

Note the use of **sentir** + definite article + (origin of scent):

| this smells of rosewater | = | **ça sent l'eau de rose** |
| Beaujolais has a scent of violet(s) | = | **le beaujolais sent la violette** |

Note the use of **à** in these examples:

| scented with rosewater | = | **parfumé à l'eau de rose** |
| to scent sth with rosewater | = | **parfumer qch à l'eau de rose** |

For shrubs and flowering plants see *Trees*.

For names of flowers used as colours (*a lilac dress, a daffodil yellow hat*), see *Colours*.

....

Fruit

Here are the names of some common types of fruit:

apple	=	**pomme** *f*
apricot	=	**abricot** *m*
banana	=	**banane** *f*
grape	=	**raisin** *m*
lemon	=	**citron** *m*
lime	=	**citron** *m* **vert**
mandarine	=	**mandarine** *f*
orange	=	**orange** *f*
peach	=	**pêche** *f*
pear	=	**poire** *f*
pineapple	=	**ananas** *m*
raisin	=	**raisin** *m* **sec**
raspberry	=	**framboise** *f*
strawberry	=	**fraise** *f*
sultana	=	**raisin** *m* **de Smyrne**
tangerine	=	**mandarine** *f*

The species and individual fruit: use of the article and of singular/plural

On the whole French uses the definite article in the same way as English to refer to the species in general:

the gooseberry is low in calories but rich in vitamin C	=	**la groseille à maquereaux est peu énergétique mais riche en vitamine C**
the raspberry keeps poorly	=	**la framboise se conserve mal**

| the strawberry is much in demand | = **la fraise se vend très bien** |
| the redcurrant grows well here | = **la groseille pousse bien par ici** |

The definite article is also used when referring to a sub-species:

| the cultivation of the cooking apple | = **la culture de la pomme à cuire** |
| the importation of the Seville orange | = **l'importation de l'orange de Séville** |

In speaking of the species using the plural, English has no article whereas French uses the definite article:

| they like oranges | = **elles aiment les oranges** |
| apples are a popular fruit | = **les pommes se vendent bien** |

Translating English compound expressions

English compounds are often translated by French expressions with **de**:

orange peel	= **de la peau d'orange**
an apple pip	= **un pépin de pomme**
a plum stone	= **un noyau de prune**
an apple core	= **un trognon de pomme**

As usual, English *X juice* = French **jus de X**, but there is some hesitation as to whether the singular or the plural is most appropriate. The singular is always safe:

lemon juice	= **jus de citron**
fruit juice	= **jus de fruit** *or* **fruits**
gooseberry juice	= **jus de groseille** *or* **groseilles**

Use the plural after **de** in the following:

| a fruit farmer | = **un producteur de fruits** |
| an orange grower | = **un producteur d'oranges** |

In types of food, **à** + definite article is a common
construction where the fruit is one ingredient:

a strawberry/an apple pie	=	**une tarte aux fraises/aux pommes**

This is especially the case when taste and flavour are
concerned:

apple sauce	=	**de la sauce à la pomme**
peach yoghurt	=	**du yaourt à la pêche**

But **de** is used, with no article, when the substance is the
only one used:

stewed apples	=	**de la compote de pommes**

and also for strong liquor:

plum/grape brandy	=	**de l'eau de vie de prune/de raisin**
pear brandy	=	**de l'alcool de poire**

For uses like *this apple* (= *this apple tree*) see *Trees*.

For expressions of colour using fruit, such as: *banana
yellow; lime green; cherry red; strawberry pink; peach-
coloured; to paint sth peach*, see *Colours*.

For *pear-shaped*, etc. see *Shapes*.

See also *Food substances*.

....

Vegetables

Here are the names of some common vegetables:

broccoli	=	**brocoli** *m*
(brussels) sprout	=	**chou** *m* **de Bruxelles**
cabbage	=	**chou** *m*
carrot	=	**carotte** *f*
cauliflower	=	**chou-fleur** *m*

cucumber	=	**concombre** *m*
leek	=	**poireau** *m*
lettuce	=	**laitue** *f* (*often referred to as* **une salade**)
onion	=	**oignon** *m*
pepper	=	**poivron** *m* (red/green: **rouge/vert**)
potato	=	**pomme** *f* **de terre** (*colloquially* **patate**)
radish	=	**radis** *m*
spinach	=	(*usually plural*) **des épinards** *mpl*
swede	=	**rutabaga** *m*
tomato	=	**tomate** *f*
turnip	=	**navet** *m*

The species and individual vegetables: use of the article and of singular/plural

On the whole French uses the definite article in the same way as English to refer to the species in general:

the cultivation of the tomato	=	**la culture de la tomate**
the potato became popular in the 18th C	=	**la pomme de terre est devenue populaire au XVIIIe**

In speaking of the species using the plural, English has no article whereas French uses the definite article:

leeks are good for you	=	**les poireaux font du bien**
our guinea-pigs love carrots	=	**nos cobayes adorent les carottes**

Both English and French distinguish between the individual vegetables and a quantity of the same vegetable when cooked:

add some tomatoes/ onions	=	**ajoutez des tomates/des oignons**

add some tomato/onion	= **ajoutez de la tomate/de l'oignon**
to cook a cauliflower	= **faire cuire un chou-fleur**
a little more cauliflower?	= **encore un peu de chou-fleur?**

But French always uses the plural for:

| this spinach | = **ces épinards** |
| to plant broccoli | = **planter des brocolis** |

And both languages use the plural for small items which keep their separate identity:

| to pick some radishes | = **récolter des radis** |

Translating English compound and complex expressions

English compounds are often translated by French expressions with **de**:

a lettuce heart	= **un cœur de laitue**
potato peelings	= **des épluchures de pommes de terre**
tomato juice	= **du jus de tomate(s)**
a celery stalk	= **une tige de céleri**

Also use **de** for dishes made of numerous pieces of the vegetable (with singular or plural as appropriate):

| celery salad | = **salade de céleri** |
| tomato soup | = **soupe de tomates** |

As usual, use **de** for English *of*:

| a clove of garlic | = **une gousse d'ail** |

Various English compound expressions concerning growing or marketing tend to have French equivalents using **de** + definite article (with singular or plural as appropriate):

| salsify cultivation | = **la culture du salsifis** |
| tomato growing | = **la culture de la tomate** *or* **des tomates** |

onion selling	= **la vente des oignons**
the radish harvest	= **la récolte des radis**

But **à** is used, as elsewhere, for flavours:

onion sauce	= **sauce à l'oignon**

See also *Food substances*.

....

Herbs and spices

Here are the names of some common herbs and spices:

basil	= **basilic** *m*
cardamom	= **cardamome** *f*
cinnamon	= **cannelle** *f*
a clove	= **clou** *m* **de girofle**
coriander	= **coriandre** *f*
garlic	= **ail** *m*
ginger	= **gingembre** *m*
marjoram	= **marjolaine** *f*
mustard	= **moutarde** *f*
oregano	= **origan** *m*
paprika	= **paprika** *m*
parsley	= **persil** *m*
pepper	= **poivre** *m*
rosemary	= **romarin** *m*
sage	= **sauge** *f*
salt	= **sel** *m*
thyme	= **thym** *m*
chili *or* chilli *or* chil(l)i pepper	= **piment** *m*

Most of the above words only exist in the singular (you do not say *basils* or *sages*). It is almost always safe to use the singular in French:

flavoured with chillis   = **parfumé au piment**
(*little red or green
things*) *and* flavoured
with chilli (*substance*)

add a few chopped chives = **ajoutez de la ciboulette hachée**

When referring to the plant used as a substance, English
tends to use the singular with no article, while French
uses the singular with the partitive article (**du/de la/
de l'**):

to plant sage	= **planter de la sauge**
to grow thyme	= **cultiver du thym**
with chopped parsley	= **avec du persil haché**
to use dried coriander	= **utiliser de la coriandre séchée**

Translating English compound and complex expressions

English compounds are often translated by French
expressions with **de**.

This is the case with second elements such as *oil, salt,
seed, powder, pepper:*

chilli powder	= **poudre** *f* **de piment** *or* **chili** *m* **en poudre**
poppy seed	= **grain** *m* **de pavot**
sesame oil	= **huile** *f* **de sésame**

Also use **de** when referring to part of a spice or herb:

a cardamon seed	= **une graine de cardamome**
a basil leaf	= **une feuille de basilic**

And, as usual, use **de** without article for English
expressions with *of*:

a sprig of thyme	= **un brin de thym**
a pinch of salt	= **une pincée de sel**

Forms with **à** + definite article are also used. This is
normal for items flavoured or scented with something or
prepared in a particular manner:

chilli sauce	= **sauce au chili**
celery salt	= **sel au céleri**

Likewise:

flavoured with garlic	= **parfumé à l'ail**

And sometimes an adjective is used as a complement
with names when referring to sub-types:

chilli pepper	= **piment rouge**
black pepper	= **poivre noir**

See also *Food substances*.

Drinks

Here are the names of some common drinks:

beer	= **bière** *f*
coffee	= **café** *m*
coke	= **coca (cola)** *m*
fruit juice	= **jus** *m* **de fruit** (orange juice = **jus d'orange**, etc.)
gin	= **gin** *m*
lemonade	= **limonade** *f*
milk	= **lait** *m*
rum	= **rhum** *m*
tea	= **thé** *m*
vodka	= **vodka** *f*
water	= **eau** *f* (mineral water = **eau minérale**)
whisky	= **whisky** *m*
wine	= **vin** *m*

French uses the definite article for general expressions
where English has no article:

I like beer	= **j'aime la bière**
the consumption of wine	= **la consommation du vin**
the sale of vodka	= **la vente de la vodka**

As usual in French, quantities are expressed using **de**:

a bottle of whisky	= **une bouteille de whisky**
two litres of milk	= **deux litres de lait**
a glass of wine	= **un verre de vin**
enough vodka	= **assez de vodka**
a lot of beer	= **beaucoup de bière**

But it is important to distinguish between a quantity in a
container (**de**) and that same container's purpose (**à**):

a cup of coffee	= **une tasse de café**
a coffee cup	= **une tasse à café**
a glass of whisky	= **un verre de whisky**
a whisky glass	= **un verre à whisky**

See also *Containers; Quantities and measurements.*

Like English, French can refer to a drink by the word for
its container:

another glass?	= **encore un verre?**

And the word for a drink can refer to *one unit of the drink.*
Gender follows that of the drink:

I'll have a coke	= **je prends un coca**
that's your third rum	= **c'est ton troisième rhum**
four coffees for table 10	= **quatre cafés pour la table dix**

For combinations of drinks, French tends not to use **et**
where English has *and*:

a gin and tonic	= **un gin tonic**
a whisky and soda	≈ **un whisky-Perrier**

Sub-types of drink

In many cases, expressions with **de** with no article are used:

China/Ceylon tea	= **thé de Chine/de Ceylan**
Colombian coffee	= **café de Colombie**
table wine	= **vin de table**
spring water	= **eau de source**

and also in the following where English has 's:

| cow's/goat's/ewe's milk | = **lait de vache/de chèvre/de brebis** |

In other cases, **de** + definite article is appropriate:

Brazilian coffee	= **café du Brésil**
Jamaican rum	= **rhum de la Jamaïque**
tap water	= **eau du robinet**

And both languages have expressions with an adjective:

| Belgian/German beer | = **bière belge/allemande** |
| Scotch/Irish whisky | = **whisky écossais/irlandais** |

Food substances

Here are the names of some common types of food:

grain	= **céréales** *fpl*
fish	= **poisson** *m*
meat	= **viande** *f*
poultry	= **volaille** *f*
vegetables	= **légumes** *mpl*
bread	= **pain** *m*
rice	= **riz** *m*
pasta	= **pâtes** *fpl*

For meat, French, like English, tends to refer to the young of the species:

| chicken | = **poulet** *m* |
| lamb | = **agneau** *m* (*and rarely* **mouton** *m* = sheep) |

Also:

| veal | = **veau** *m* |

but:

| beef | = **bœuf** *m* |
| pork | = **porc** *m* |

French uses the definite article to refer to the substance in general; use the plural if the word is plural:

I like beef	= **j'aime le bœuf**
they like carrots/ spinach	= **elles aiment les carottes/les épinards**
salmon is expensive	= **le saumon est très cher**

And the definite article is used in both languages for specific reference:

| how much is the salmon? | = **le saumon est à combien?** |
| is the pasta home-made? | = **les pâtes sont faites maison?** |

But the partitive article is used for expressions referring to imprecise quantities:

to eat chicken	= **manger du poulet**
served with rice	= **servi avec du riz**
in this dish there's plaice, cod,...	= **dans ce plat, il y a du carrelet, de la morue,...**

As usual, French uses **de** with many quantity expressions:

a lot of meat	= **beaucoup de viande**
not much bread	= **peu de pain**
a pound of onions	= **une livre d'oignons**

And **de** alone is used, as usual, after a negative:

| they don't eat meat | = **ils ne mangent pas de viande** |

As in English, there may be a need to distinguish
between small items (plural) and parts or slices of larger
items (partitive):

three more trout (*three separate fish*)	=	**encore trois truites**
some more cod? (*part of one fish*)	=	**encore du cabillaud?**
some more sprouts (*several items*)	=	**encore quelques choux de Bruxelles**
some more cabbage? (*part of a dish*)	=	**encore du chou?**

Both languages have words to specify smaller quantities
of a larger item. These usually include **de** in French,
whether English has *of* or uses a compound expression:

a chicken wing	=	**une aile de poulet**
a joint of lamb	=	**un gigot d'agneau**
a slice of ham	=	**une tranche de jambon**
a pork cutlet	=	**une côte(lette) de porc**
a lamb chop	=	**une côte(lette) d'agneau**
a salmon steak	=	**un steak de saumon**
salmon fillets	=	**des filets de saumon**
salmon eggs	=	**des œufs de saumon**

And this also applies to expressions with -*'s* in English:

lamb's liver	=	**foie *m* d'agneau**
goat's milk	=	**lait *m* de chèvre**

Although **de** is most usual when translating English
compounds, **à** + definite article is often preferred in cases
where the contents of an item are referred to:

a steak and kidney pie	=	**une tourte au bœuf et aux rognons**
an apple flan/tart	=	**une tarte aux pommes**
a bran loaf	=	**un pain au son**
salmon tagliatelle	=	**des tagliatelles au saumon**

a curry/mushroom sauce	=	**une sauce au curry/aux champignons**
a ham sandwich	=	**un sandwich au jambon**
onion soup	=	**de la soupe à l'oignon**

This principle extends to accompanying contents:

| beef and carrots | = | **bœuf** *m* **aux carottes** |
| salad with basil | = | **salade** *f* **au basilic** |

And **à** without article is used when purpose is involved:

| batter | = | **pâte** *f* **à beignets** *or* **à frire** |

The human body

Body parts and organs

Here are the names of the main body parts:

ankle	=	**cheville** *f*
arm	=	**bras** *m*
back	=	**dos** *m*
breast	=	**sein** *m*
cheek	=	**joue** *f*
chest	=	**poitrine** *f*
chin	=	**menton** *m*
ear	=	**oreille** *f*
elbow	=	**coude** *m*
eye	=	**œil** *m* (*plural* **yeux**)
finger	=	**doigt** *m*
foot	=	**pied** *m*
forehead	=	**front** *m*
hair	=	**cheveux** *mpl*
hand	=	**main** *f*
head	=	**tête** *f*
knee	=	**genou** *m*
leg	=	**jambe** *f*
lip	=	**lèvre** *f*
mouth	=	**bouche** *f*
neck	=	**cou** *m*
nose	=	**nez** *m*
shoulder	=	**épaule** *f*
tongue	=	**langue** *f*

Others:

bone	=	**os** *m*
brain	=	**cerveau** *m*
heart	=	**cœur** *m*
kidney	=	**rein** *m*
liver	=	**foie** *m*
lung	=	**poumon** *m*
muscle	=	**muscle** *m*
skin	=	**peau** *f*
stomach	=	**estomac** *m*

Note the use of **à** in the following:

a boy with long hair *or* a long-haired boy	= **un garçon aux cheveux longs**
the girl with blue eyes *or* the blue-eyed girl	= **la fille aux yeux bleus**
a girl with blond hair *or* a blond-haired girl	= **une fille à la chevelure blonde**
a man with a red nose *or* a red-nosed man	= **un homme au nez rouge**

Translating English possessives

The main difficulty is to know when to use a possessive (**mon/ma/mes**, etc.) and when to use an article. There are no absolute rules here, but the following remarks should by useful.

Where it is clear who owns the body part, French prefers the definite article:

he raised his hand	= **il a levé la main**
put your hands up!	= **haut les mains!**
she closed her eyes	= **elle a fermé les yeux**

The definite article is also used in common constructions for describing people:

his hair is long *or* he has long hair	= **il a les cheveux longs**

| her eyes are blue *or* she has blue eyes *or* she is blue-eyed | = **elle a les yeux bleus** |
| his nose is red *or* he has a red nose | = **il a le nez rouge** |

When the 'possessor' of the part is the subject of the verb, French prefers to use a reflexive verb and the definite article:

she has broken her leg	= **elle s'est cassé la jambe**
he was rubbing his hands	= **il se frottait les mains**
she was holding her head	= **elle se tenait la tête**

When the part belongs to someone other than the subject, the possessive may be used, though the definite article is more common:

| I caressed his hair | = **j'ai caressé ses cheveux** *or* **je lui ai caressé les cheveux** |
| you stepped on his hands | = **tu as marché sur ses doigts** *or* **tu lui as marché sur les doigts** |

Note that in the above examples the 'possessor' is referred to by an indirect object pronoun, as also in:

| she broke his leg | = **elle lui a cassé la jambe** |
| the stone split her lip | = **la pierre lui a fendu la lèvre** |

Note the use of both the definite article and the possessive in the following:

| she ran her hand over my forehead | = **elle a passé la main sur mon front** |

Where the action of the verb is not usually associated with parts of the body, and where the construction using a pronoun is not possible, French prefers the possessive:

made with her (own) hands	= **fabriqué de ses mains**
they won't show their hair	= **elles refusent de montrer leurs cheveux**
the child rushed into her arms	= **l'enfant s'est précipité dans ses bras**

The possessive is normal after most prepositions, whoever the 'possessor' is:

he was attacked despite his white hair	= **il s'est fait agresser malgré ses cheveux blancs**
beneath her white hair she is still the girl I loved	= **sous ses cheveux blancs elle demeure la jeune fille que j'ai aimée**
Jacques, with his thick, short hair, was easily recognizable	= **Jacques, avec ses cheveux drus et courts, était facilement reconnaissable**
he grips his face between his hands	= **il serre son visage entre ses mains**
the constant trembling of her hands	= **le tremblement constant de ses mains**

In some cases, article and possessive are both possible:

with scratches on her hands and face	= **avec des griffures sur ses mains et (sur) son visage** or **avec des griffures sur les mains et (sur) le visage**

The possessive is also used in figurative expressions such as:

our fate is in his hands	= **notre sort est entre ses mains**
the human race holds its fate in its (own) hands	= **l'humanité tient son sort entre ses mains**
to fall into their hands	= **tomber entre leurs mains**

The possessive is also usual if the term comes first in a sentence:

his hands were trembling	=	**ses mains tremblaient** *or* (*more colloquial*) **il avait les mains qui tremblaient**
his hands are stained with blood	=	**ses mains sont tachées de sang** *or* (*more colloquial*) **il a les mains tachées de sang**
her hair has turned completely white	=	**ses cheveux sont devenus tout blancs**

Note the following useful expressions for temporary states:

| his leg is broken | = | **il a la jambe cassée** |
| the man with the broken leg | = | **l'homme à la jambe cassée** |

but:

| a man with a broken leg | = | **un homme avec une jambe cassée** |

....

Illnesses, aches and pains

Here are the names of some common complaints and illnesses:

Aids	=	**sida** *m*
appendicitis	=	**appendicite** *f*
arthritis	=	**arthrite** *f*
asthma	=	**asthme** *m*
bronchitis	=	**bronchite** *f*
cancer	=	**cancer** *m*
chicken pox	=	**varicelle** *f*
cold	=	**rhume** *m*
cough	=	**toux** *f*
diarrhoea	=	**diarrhée** *f*

flu	=	**grippe** *f*
German measles	=	**rubéole** *f*
hay fever	=	**rhume** *m* **des foins**
hepatitis	=	**hépatite** *f*
malaria	=	**malaria** *f*
measles	=	**rougeole** *f*
mumps	=	**oreillons** *mpl*
pneumonia	=	**pneumonie** *f*
rhumatism	=	**rhumatismes** *mpl*
scarlet fever	=	**scarlatine** *f*
smallpox	=	**variole** *f*
tetanus	=	**tétanos** *m*
whooping cough	=	**coqueluche** *f*

It hurts!

Note the distinction between **avoir mal à** + definite article (a specific pain) and **un/le mal de** (the condition in general):

where does it hurt?	=	**où avez-vous mal?**
my leg hurts	=	**j'ai mal à la jambe** *or* **ma jambe me fait mal**
his ears hurt	=	**il a mal aux oreilles**
he has a pain in his leg	=	**il a mal à la jambe**
his head was aching	=	**il avait mal à la tête**
to have toothache	=	**avoir mal aux dents**

but:

| backache | = | **le mal de dos** |

and (with adjective):

| to have frightful headaches | = | **avoir d'affreux maux de tête** |

Do not confuse the following:

| that hurt him | = **cela lui a fait mal** |
| that harmed him | = **cela lui a fait du mal** |

Accidents

| she has broken her leg | = **elle s'est cassé la jambe** |
| she has sprained her ankle | = **elle s'est foulé la cheville** |

For other expressions involving parts of the body, see *Body parts and organs.*

Chronic conditions

French often uses **fragile** for such conditions. Note the use of the definite article:

to have a weak heart	= **avoir le cœur fragile**
to have kidney trouble	= **avoir les reins fragiles**
to have a bad back	= **avoir le dos fragile**

Use of articles

French uses the definite article with most infectious diseases, including childhood illnesses:

to have flu	= **avoir la grippe**
to have measles	= **avoir la rougeole**
to have malaria	= **avoir la malaria**
to have Aids	= **avoir le sida**

But the indefinite article is preferred for some illnesses affecting specific parts of the body and for words ending in **-ite**:

to have cancer	= **avoir un cancer**
to suffer from lung cancer	= **souffrir d'un cancer des poumons**
to have pneumonia	= **avoir une pneumonie**

to have a stomach ulcer	=	**avoir un ulcère à l'estomac**
to have hepatitis	=	**avoir une hépatite**
to have meningitis	=	**avoir une méningite**

For certain generalized conditions French tends to use the partitive:

to have rheumatism	=	**avoir des rhumatismes**
to have emphysema	=	**avoir de l'emphysème**
to have asthma	=	**avoir de l'asthme**
to have arthritis	=	**avoir de l'arthrite**

but:

to have hay fever	=	**avoir le rhume des foins**

Where the illness as a phenomenon is referred to, the definite article is used:

mortality due to hepatitis	=	**la mortalité due à l'hépatite**
problems caused by rheumatism	=	**des problèmes occasionnés par les rhumatismes**
to study cancer of the liver	=	**étudier le cancer du foie**

Where there is an appropriate adjective, French may prefer this construction:

to have asthma	=	**être asthmatique**
to have epilepsy	=	**être épileptique**

Other expressions

When referring to people suffering from conditions, it is often possible to use an adjective as a noun:

someone with cancer *or* a cancer patient	=	**un cancéreux/une cancéreuse**

But it is always safe to use **qui a/ont**:

someone with Aids	=	**quelqu'un qui a le sida**

people with malaria   = **ceux** *or* **les gens qui ont la malaria**

Falling ill

Verbs such as **attraper** and **contracter** are used with the appropriate article:

to catch malaria   = **attraper la malaria**
to catch bronchitis   = **attraper une bronchite**
to contract pneumonia   = **contracter une pneumonie**
to catch a cold   = **attraper un rhume**
to contract Aids   = **contracter le sida**

attack, bout and *fit*

The above can all be translated by **crise**:

a bout of malaria   = **une crise de malaria**
an asthma attack   = **une crise d'asthme**
an epileptic fit   = **une crise d'épilepsie**

Treatment

Note the use of **contre** to translate *for*:

to be treated for polio   = **se faire soigner contre la polio**
to take something for a   = **prendre quelque chose contre** *or*
  cough   **pour la toux**

contre is also used for some English compound expressions:

malaria tablets   = **des cachets contre la malaria**
to have a tetanus injection = **se faire vacciner contre le tétanos**

And **contre** also (as usual) translates *against*:

to be vaccinated against   = **se faire vacciner contre la variole**
  smallpox

But note the construction with **opérer**:

to be operated on for   = **être opéré d'un cancer**
  cancer

to operate on someone = **opérer quelqu'un de l'appendicite**
  for appendicitis

Translating English compounds:

Sub-types of illnesses or conditions tend to use **de** +
definite article:

breast cancer = **le cancer du sein**

stomach cancer = **le cancer de l'estomac**

to have cancer of the = **avoir un cancer du foie**
  liver

In other compounds, where the word for the illness or
condition comes first, **de** alone is more usual:

an Aids epidemic = **une épidémie de sida**

our first case of cholera = **notre premier cas de choléra**

pneumonia sufferers = **des malades atteints de pneumonie**

....

Medicines

Here are the names for common forms of medicines:

ampoule/phial = **ampoule** *f*

capsule = **gélule** *f*

dose = **dose** *f*

injection = **injection** *f*

medicine = **médicament** *m*

pill = **pilule** *f*

syrup = **sirop** *m*

tablet = **cachet** *m or* **comprimé** *m*

Articles

Like English, French distinguishes between an object
(definite or indefinite article) and a substance (partitive
article):

to take a tablet/a pill = **prendre un comprimé/une pilule**

to take (some) aspirin	=	**prendre de l'aspirine**
I take paracetamol for headaches	=	**je prends du paracétamol pour le mal de tête**
he's taking these tablets for diarrhoea	=	**il prend ces comprimés pour la diarrhée**

To be on ...

For some strong substances, **sous** is used:

| he's on heroin | = | **il est sous héroïne** |
| they put me on cortisone | = | **ils m'ont mis sous cortisone** |

Translating English compounds

When translating English compounds, French tends to use **de** for content and **à** + definite article for treatment:

| an aspirin (tablet) | = | **un comprimé d'aspirine** |
| a morphine injection | = | **une injection de morphine** |

but:

| cortisone treatment | = | **traitement à la cortisone** |

Social roles and organizations

Religions, beliefs, and religious services

Religions and beliefs

Here are some words for faiths and beliefs. In general, English *-ism* = French **-isme** (always masculine). Note the use of lower-case initial letters in French:

Faiths

Animism	=	**animisme** *m*
Buddhism	=	**bouddhisme** *m*
Christianity	=	**christianisme** *m* (*note that* **chrétienté** *f* = Christendom)
Hinduism	=	**hindouisme** *m*
Islam	=	**islam** *m*
Judaism	=	**judaïsme** *m*
Shintoism	=	**shintoïsme** *m*
Taoism	=	**taoïsme** *m*

Beliefs

Atheism	=	**athéisme** *m*
Humanism	=	**humanisme** *m*
Marxist-Leninism	=	**marxisme-léninisme** *m*

French uses the definite article to refer to faiths, where English has no article:

to practise Christianity	=	**pratiquer le christianisme**
to convert someone to Islam	=	**convertir quelqu'un à l'islam**
to believe in Buddhism	=	**croire au bouddhisme**

Do not use **un/une** or **des** in French after **être/devenir**. (See also *Shops, trades, jobs, and professions*, etc.):

she is a Marxist	= **elle est marxiste**
Sylvie and Marc are Christians	= **Sylvie et Marc sont chrétiens**
to become a Muslim	= **devenir musulman/musulmane**

But when an adjective is introduced the article is obligatory, and **il(s)/elle(s)** are replaced by **ce**:

| she is a fervent Hindu | = **c'est une hindoue fervente** |
| they are Tibetan Buddhists | = **ce sont des bouddhistes tibétains** |

But usage is a little undecided in the following:

| I am a practising Catholic | = **je suis catholique pratiquant(e)** |

In both English and French, there are a number of identical forms used for a person holding beliefs and for the related adjective:

an atheist	= **un/une athée**
atheist convictions	= **des convictions athées**
a Christian	= **un chrétien/une chrétienne**
Christian teaching	= **des enseignements chrétiens**
a Muslim	= **un musulman/une musulmane**
Muslim families	= **des familles musulmanes**
a Jew	= **un juif/une juive**
Jewish rites	= **des rites juifs**

Religious services, etc.

Here are the names of some religious services and other events:

baptism	= **baptême** *m*
burial	= **enterrement** *m*
christening	= **baptême** *m*

communion	=	**communion** f
funeral	=	**funérailles** fpl
marriage	=	**mariage** m
mass	=	**messe** f
prayers	=	**prière** f
wedding	=	**mariage** m/**noces** fpl

Where English uses the word with no article, French prefers to use the definite article:

to go to mass	=	**aller à la messe**
to take communion	=	**recevoir la communion**
to go to prayers	=	**aller à la prière**
to practise infant baptism	=	**pratiquer le baptême des enfants**

Most English compound expressions are translated by French expressions with **de**:

wedding breakfast	=	**repas** m **de noces** (*similarly*: **repas de communion; repas de baptême**)
christening robe	=	**robe** f **de baptême**
wedding dress	=	**robe** f **de mariage**

....

Festivals

Here are the names of some common festivals, etc:

Some involve one word in French:

Christmas	=	**Noël** (*generally masculine, but see below*)
Easter	=	**Pâques** fpl

Others require the article (**la** for saints' days) and often include phrases such as **le jour de**:

| Passover | = | **la Pâque juive** |

Whitsun	= **la Pentecôte**
All Saints' Day	= **la Toussaint**
Ascension Day	= **(le jour de) l'Ascension** *f*
Good Friday	= **le vendredi saint**
Labour Day	= **la fête du Travail**
New Year's Eve	= **la Saint-Sylvestre**
Palm Sunday	= **les Rameaux** *or* **le dimanche des Rameaux**

Happy

| Happy Christmas | = **joyeux Noël** |

But the French for *Easter* is plural, so:

| Happy Easter | = **joyeuses Pâques** (*rarely used*) |
| Happy Birthday | = **bon anniversaire** *or* **joyeux anniversaire** |

Translating *at, on, for, over*

For *at*, **à** is used, often with the definite article:

at Christmas	= **à Noël** *or* **à la Noël** (*though* **Noël** *is masculine*)
at Midsummer (= *on St John's Day*)	= **à la Saint-Jean**
at Easter	= **à Pâques**

Sometimes constructions with **le jour de/la veille de/le lendemain de** or **pour** are used instead of **à**:

| we met at Whitsun | = **nous nous sommes rencontrés à la Pentecôte** (*or* **le jour de la Pentecôte**) |
| they'll be here at Easter | = **ils seront là pour Pâques** |

For *on*, French often uses no preposition at all.

Note that many expressions are feminine, where **la = la fête de**; this includes all saints' days, whether the saint is

male or female and whatever the gender of the name of
the festival:

on St Andrew's Day	=	**le jour de la Saint-André** (*or* **à la Saint-André**)
it snowed on Christmas Eve	=	**il a neigé la veille de Noël**
the service on Palm Sunday	=	**l'office du jour des Rameaux** (*or* **pour les Rameaux**)
he was dismissed (on) the day before Good Friday	=	**il a été renvoyé la veille du vendredi saint**
she left on New Year's Eve	=	**elle est partie le jour de la Saint-Sylvestre**
he died on Easter Sunday	=	**il est mort le dimanche de Pâques**

For (purpose) is usually translated by **pour**, but
sometimes by **à**:

I got this present for Christmas	=	**j'ai eu ce cadeau pour** *or* **à Noël**
we give people eggs for Easter	=	**nous offrons des œufs pour Pâques**

For and *over* (time) are translated by **pour**:

we had a lot of people for Christmas	=	**on a eu beaucoup de gens pour Noël**
we're going for a cruise over Easter	=	**on va faire une croisière pour Pâques**
it snowed over Christmas	=	**il a neigé pour Noël**

For English compound expressions, French (as usual)
links two nouns with **de**:

Christmas turkey	=	**dinde de Noël**
Christmas greetings	=	**vœux de Noël**
Christmas card/present	=	**carte/cadeau de Noël**
Easter egg	=	**œuf de Pâques**

And the definite article is also needed in the following:

| Passover celebrations | = **fêtes de la Pâque juive** |
| Midsummer firework display | = **feu d'artifice de la Saint-Jean** |

Sometimes a separate expression exists:

| Holy week | = **semaine sainte** |
| Easter candle | = **cierge pascal** (*or* **cierge de Pâques**) |

Birthdays

The usual word for *birthday* is **anniversaire,** as in the following expression:

| when's your birthday? | = **c'est quand, ton anniversaire?** (*colloquial*) |

Expressions with **ans** also exist:

I was given it for my tenth birthday	= **c'était un cadeau pour mes dix ans** *or* **pour mon dixième anniversaire**
I was given a watch for my twenty-first	= **on m'a offert une montre pour mes vingt-et-un ans**
come to the party for Fred's sixtieth	= **viens fêter les soixante ans de Fred**

....

Institutions

Here are the names of some common institutions:

bank	= **banque** *f*
factory	= **usine** *f*
hospital	= **hôpital** *m*
museum	= **musée** *m*
office	= **bureau** *m*
school	= **école** *f*

(In France, Junior secondary school is **le collège**; Senior secondary school is **le lycée**.)

Translating *to*, *in*, *at*

Where English has *to/in/at* (+ definite article), French
normally uses **à** (+ definite article) in all cases:

to go to school/to hospital	= **aller à l'école/à l'hôpital**
to go to the bank/to work at the bank	= **aller à la banque/travailler à la banque**
to go to the museum/to work in the museum	= **aller au musée/travailler au musée**

For *school, hospital* French makes no difference between:

to go to school/to the school	= **aller à l'école**
to stay in hospital/in the hospital	= **rester à l'hôpital**

When the indefinite article is used, *in, at* are usually
translated as **dans**:

she works in a factory/in an office	= **elle travaille dans une usine/dans un bureau**
he teaches at a Senior Secondary School	= **il enseigne dans un lycée**

Most English compound expressions are translated by
French expressions with **de**:

factory worker	= **ouvrier/ouvrière** *m/f* **d'usine**
office worker	= **employé/employée** *m/f* **de bureau**
hospital director	= **directeur** *m* **d'hôpital**
museum curator	= **conservateur** *m* **de musée**

Ministries and ministers

In general, whatever the British and American terms
are, French uses **le ministère/le ministre de** + definite
article + name of ministry, e.g.:

British ministries and ministers

the Board of Trade	= **le ministère du Commerce et de l'Industrie**
the Foreign Office	= **le ministère des Affaires étrangères**
the Home Secretary	= **le ministre de l'Intérieur**
the Secretary of State for Defence	= **le ministre de la Défense**

US Departments, Secretaries, etc.

the State Department	= **le ministère des Affaires étrangères**
the Pentagon	= **le ministère de la Défense**
the Attorney General	= **le ministre de la Justice**
the Secretary of Labor	= **le ministre du Travail**
the Commerce Department	= **le ministère du Commerce**

For is translated as **de** with **ministre** but as **à** with **secrétaire d'État**:

the Minister for Health	= **le ministre de la Santé**
the Secretary of State for Transport	= **le secrétaire d'État aux Transports**

Gender

Part of the move to create or allow feminine forms where none have previously existed involves making **ministre** a word of either gender. Traditionally, however, a female minister has been referred to as **Madame le ministre**. She is normally referred to as **elle**.

See also *Forms of address*.

Shops, trades, jobs, and professions

Here are the names of some common jobs and professions:

architect	= **architecte** *m* or *f*

baker	=	**boulanger/boulangère** *m/f*
butcher	=	**boucher/bouchère** *m/f*
clerk, office worker	=	**employé/employée** *m/f* **(de bureau)**
dentist	=	**dentiste** *m* or *f*
doctor	=	**docteur** *m*, **médecin** *m*
lawyer	=	**avocat/avocate** *m/f*
teacher	=	**enseignant/enseignante** *m/f*

Note: **professeur** is mainly for teachers at secondary schools or at universities; primary teachers have traditionally been called **instituteur/institutrice**. Their official title is now **professeur des écoles**.

worker	=	**ouvrier/ouvrière** *m/f*

When referring to professions and trades in a general sense follow the usual pattern, using a definite article in French where English has none:

to study surgery	=	**étudier la chirurgie**
the importance of bakery	=	**l'importance de la boulangerie**
to go in for architecture	=	**se lancer dans l'architecture**

People and their jobs

French does not use the indefinite article after **être** or **devenir**:

he's a doctor	=	**il est médecin**
she's a teacher	=	**elle est enseignante**
they are architects	=	**ils sont architectes**

But when an adjective is introduced, the indefinite article is obligatory and **il(s)/elle(s)** are replaced by **ce**:

she's an excellent barrister	=	**c'est une excellente avocate**
he's a very fine dentist	=	**c'est un très bon dentiste**
they are conscientious workers	=	**ce sont des ouvriers consciencieux**

| they are very poor clerks | = **ce sont de très mauvais employés** |

French does not use the indefinite article after **comme**:

| I work as a chemist | = **je travaille comme pharmacien/pharmacienne** |
| she is really good as an architect | = **elle est vraiment bien comme architecte** (*colloquial*) |

Places of trade or work
Specific names for some places of work

Note the use of **cabinet** for the offices of architects, dentists, doctors, auctioneers (**commissaire priseur**), lawyers (including **notaires**).

she works for an architect	= **elle travaille pour un architecte**
she works at a lawyer's	= **elle travaille chez un avocat**
she works for/at an auctioneer's practice	= **elle travaille pour un cabinet de commissaire priseur** *or* **elle travaille dans un cabinet de commissaire priseur**

chez or *à*

French distinguishes (for example) *the baker's* from *the bakery*; **chez** is used with people, **à** with establishments.

| you'll get it at the baker's | = **vous le trouverez chez le boulanger** |
| you'll get it at the bakery | = **vous le trouverez à la boulangerie** |

Similarly:

| to go to the butcher's/ chemist's | = **se rendre chez le boucher/le pharmacien** |
| to go to the butcher's shop/the chemist's shop | = **se rendre à la boucherie/à la pharmacie** |

chez is also used in the following cases relating to professions...

to go to the doctor's/ lawyer's/dentist's	= **aller chez le docteur/l'avocat/le dentiste**

...and with proper names applied to places of work or business:

I got it at Jenner's	= **je l'ai eu chez Jenner**
she works at Smith's	= **elle travaille chez Smith**

Note that **chez** also means *at the house/home of* so that some of the above examples can be ambiguous.

English compound expressions are often translated by French expressions using **de**:

a bank manager	= **un directeur d'agence bancaire**
a lawyer's clerk	= **un clerc de notaire**

Artists and their works

Here are some names of artists, etc.:

artist	= **artiste** *m/f*
draughtsman	= **dessinateur/dessinatrice** *m/f*
engraver	= **graveur** *m*
illustrator	= **illustrateur/illustratrice** *m/f*
lithographer	= **lithographe** *m/f*
painter	= **peintre** *m*
potter	= **potier** *m*
sculptor, sculptress	= **sculpteur** *m*

Note the following words ending in **-iste**:

landscape painter	= **paysagiste** *m/f*
portrait painter	= **portraitiste** *m/f*
watercolourist	= **aquarelliste** *m/f*

The list above shows that some words such as **peintre** and **sculpteur** have no feminine form. There is a move towards saying **une bonne peintre** when referring to a woman but such usage is neither officially recognized nor totally accepted. Usage also varies as between countries (e.g. between France and Quebec).

As with professions generally, the indefinite article is not needed after **être** or **devenir**:

| he's a painter | = **il est peintre** |
| Sophie is a lithographer | = **Sophie est lithographe** |

But when an adjective is introduced, the indefinite article is obligatory and **il(s)/elle(s)** are replaced by **ce**:

she's an excellent artist	= **c'est un excellent peintre**
he's a very fine sculptor	= **c'est un très bon sculpteur**
they are professional artists	= **ce sont des artistes professionnels**
they are very poor draughtsmen	= **ce sont de très mauvais dessinateurs**

Both languages can use the same word for the creative act and the object created.

For the act, English uses no article, whereas French uses the definite article:

| to learn engraving (the act) | = **apprendre la gravure** |
| to study sculpture | = **étudier la sculpture** |

For the object, the two languages use parallel articles:

| to buy an engraving | = **acheter une gravure** |
| I like this sculpture | = **j'aime bien cette sculpture** |

Similar patterns work for:

| illustration | = **illustration** *f* |

| painting | = **peinture** f (*the object can also be* **tableau** m) |
| drawing | = **dessin** m |

In some cases, English has one word where French has separate words for the act and the object:

| etching | = **gravure** f à l'eau forte (*act*); **eau-forte** f (*object*) |

Sometimes it is the other way round:

| lithography *and* lithograph | = **lithographie** f |
| pottery *and* piece of pottery | = **poterie** f |

Also:

| portrait | = **portrait** m |
| portraiture | = **portrait** m *or* **art** m du portrait |

Note that French has no equivalent for *a piece of*:

| a piece of pottery | = **une poterie** |
| a piece of sculpture | = **une sculpture** |

There is no fixed pattern for the translation of English compound words. Sometimes **de** is used:

| picture gallery | = **galerie** f de peinture |

But **à** is appropriate to indicate purpose:

| sketch pad | = **bloc** m à dessin |

Subjects of study

Here are the words for some common subjects. Note that French subjects normally take a lower-case initial letter. They are all feminine except the names of languages:

Biology	= **biologie** *f*
Botany	= **botanique** *f*
Chemistry	= **chimie** *f*
English	= **anglais** *m*
French	= **français** *m*
Geography	= **géographie** *f*
History	= **histoire** *f*
Mathematics	= **mathématiques** *fpl*
Music	= **musique** *f*
Physical Education	= **éducation** *f* **physique et sportive (EPS)**
Physics	= **physique** *f*
Religious Education	= **instruction** *f* **religieuse**
Sociology	= **sociologie** *f*

Where English uses no article, French usually uses the definite article:

to take Biology	= **choisir la biologie (comme matière)**
to learn Physics	= **apprendre la physique**
to study Chemistry	= **étudier la chimie**
to study Maths	= **étudier les maths**

but:

to do Maths	= **faire des maths**

Note the use of **en** in expressions such as the following:

to be good at Geography	= **être bon en géographie**
to be bad/weak at Physics	= **être mauvais/faible en physique**
to do well in English	= **avoir de bonnes notes en anglais**

As in other areas of French, expressions with **de** (with no article) are common when translating English compound expressions:

a Chemistry textbook	= **un manuel de chimie**

the French lesson	=	**le cours de français**
the English teacher	=	**le professeur d'anglais**
a Chemistry practical	=	**des travaux pratiques de chimie**
a History exam	=	**une épreuve d'histoire**
to write a Politics essay	=	**rédiger une dissertation de politique**

But note the further possibility of **en** in the following:

to submit a History thesis	=	**présenter une thèse d'histoire** or **en histoire**
to do a Geography project	=	**faire un mémoire de géographie** or **en géographie**
to have a degree in Mathematics	=	**avoir un diplôme de mathématiques** or **être diplômé en mathématiques**

Games and sports

Here are the names of some sports and games.

Sports

basketball	=	**basket** *m*
football	=	**football** *m*
handball	=	**handball** *m*
horse riding	=	**équitation** *f*
rugby	=	**rugby** *m*
swimming	=	**natation** *f*
tennis	=	**tennis** *m*
volleyball	=	**volley-ball** *m*

Games

billiards	=	**billard** *m*
bridge	=	**bridge** *m*
cards	=	**cartes** *fpl*
chess	=	**échecs** *mpl*

hide-and-seek	= **cache-cache** *m*
leapfrog	= **saute-mouton** *m*
marbles	= **billes** *fpl*

Where English uses no article, French normally uses the definite article:

we like football	= **nous aimons le football**
to learn chess	= **apprendre les échecs**
the rules of bridge	= **les règles du bridge**

Note that **jouer** is constructed with **à** + definite article in this sense (but see also *Musical instruments*):

| to play volleyball | = **jouer au volley-ball** |
| to play marbles | = **jouer aux billes** |

But French compound nouns of games like **saute-mouton** do *not* use the definite article:

| to play (at) leapfrog | = **jouer à saute-mouton** |
| to like hide-and-seek | = **aimer jouer à cache-cache** |

Expressions with **à** + (usually) definite article are common in a number of other constructions:

to play bridge with X against Y	= **jouer au bridge avec X contre Y**
to beat someone at chess	= **battre quelqu'un aux échecs**
to win at tennis	= **gagner au tennis**
to lose at marbles	= **perdre aux billes**
to be good at basketball	= **être bon au basket**
to play rugby well/badly	= **bien/mal jouer au rugby**

But note:

| to go in for horse riding | = **faire du cheval** |
| to go in for swimming | = **faire de la natation** |

Most compound English expressions are translated by French expressions with **de**:

a bridge club	=	**un club de bridge**
a bridge player	=	**un joueur de bridge** (*also* **un bridgeur**)
a football pitch	=	**un terrain de football**
a tennis court	=	**un court de tennis**
a card game	=	**un jeu de cartes** (*also means* a pack of cards)
a bridge champion	=	**un champion de bridge**
the French tennis champion	=	**le champion de France de tennis**
the German handball championship	=	**le championnat d'Allemagne de hand-ball**

Medals

the gold medal	=	**la médaille d'or**

French cannot use a shorter form:

to go for gold	=	**viser la médaille d'or**
to win the silver	=	**gagner la médaille d'argent**
to hope at least for the bronze	=	**espérer gagner au moins la médaille de bronze**

See also *Metals*.

....

Forms of address

Speaking to people

French does not use surnames:

good morning, Mr Jones	=	**bonjour, monsieur** (*note lower-case* m *when written*)
good evening, Mrs Brown	=	**bonsoir, madame**
excuse me, Miss Smith	=	**excusez-moi, mademoiselle**

There is therefore no difference in normal French usage between *Sir, Madam* and *Mr Smith, Mrs Jones*.

Note that French colleagues (especially male) often avoid being on first-name terms and use surnames or sometimes other expressions like **cher ami, mon vieux**.

Titles

As in English, some titles are used in French without any other expression (such as **monsieur le**):

| good morning, Doctor | = | **bonjour, docteur** |
| good-bye, Professor | = | **au revoir, professeur** |

Note that lawyers of both sexes are addressed as **maître**.

For other titles, a preceding **monsieur, madame** is needed:

good morning, sir (*to the headteacher of a lycée*)	=	**bonjour, monsieur le proviseur**
thank you, your Honour (*to a judge*)	=	**je vous remercie, monsieur le juge** (*or* **monsieur le président** *if the judge is sitting with others*)
good-bye, Father (*to the parish priest*)	=	**au revoir, monsieur le curé**

ROYALTY/AMBASSADORS

When addressing such personages directly, **votre** is not necessary:

good morning, your Majesty	=	**bonjour, Majesté**
good morning, your Excellency	=	**bonjour, Excellence**
good morning, your Highness	=	**bonjour, Altesse**

votre is only used in full sentences and to avoid saying **vous**:

| if your Highness would agree to... | = | **si votre Altesse voulait bien...** |

CHURCH DIGNITARIES

As with the nobility, you need to 'negotiate' the way to address people, but, technically, you should use the following:

- to priests: **mon père**
- to nuns: **ma sœur**
- to monks: **mon frère**
- to Protestant ministers: **monsieur le pasteur** or simply **pasteur**
- to bishops and archbishops: **monseigneur**

Note that the parish priest is both addressed and referred to as **monsieur le curé**. The form **monsieur l'abbé** is for priests who have no parish (e.g. those teaching).

Where there is no accepted feminine form say **Madame le X**:

good morning, ma'am   = **bonjour, madame le proviseur** (*or* **madame le juge** *or other title*)

The following feminine forms do exist: **madame la présidente, madame la directrice, madame la colonelle.** This is an area which is currently changing, and where French usage is not always the same as (for example) Quebec usage. You will need to ask what is acceptable.

Referring to people

Use **monsieur** etc. with the surname, in a way similar to English (but note the use of lower-case initial letters):

Mr Dupont is here   = **monsieur Dupont est là**
Mrs Zahn has arrived   = **madame Zahn est arrivée**
Miss Lelong has left   = **mademoiselle Lelong est partie**

There is no equivalent for **Ms**. If in doubt use **madame**.

For other titles include **le/la** (again, note lower-case initial letters):

Dr Yalta has phoned	=	**le docteur Yalta a téléphoné**
Princess Sandra wants a divorce	=	**la princesse Sandra demande le divorce**
Count Metternich laughed	=	**le comte Metternich a ri**

Letter formulae

In formal letter writing, you should always give people their title (if you know it), preceded by **Madame/Monsieur**, e.g. **Madame le ministre, Monsieur le président**. Never precede such expressions by **cher/chère**.

Note that, in the final paragraph (**formule de clôture**), the form used at the beginning should reappear exactly, e.g.:

Je vous prie de croire, madame le ministre, à l'expression…

Veuillez agréer, monsieur le président, l'expression…

See also *Military ranks and titles*, below.

Military ranks and titles

Here is a selection of ranks:

admiral	=	**amiral** *m*
captain	=	**capitaine** *m*
colonel	=	**colonel** *m*
corporal	=	**caporal** *m*
flight-lieutenant	=	**capitaine** *m* (de l'armée de l'air)
general	=	**général** *m*
lieutenant	=	**lieutenant** *m*
major	=	**commandant** *m*
sergeant	=	**sergent** *m*
squadron leader	=	**commandant** *m* (de l'armée de l'air)
warrant officer	=	**adjudant** *m*

Feminine forms of ranks

Historically, **la colonelle** was the colonel's wife and **la générale** was the general's wife. These words can now be used for ranks occupied by women, but the masculine forms still tend to predominate.

As with other professions (see *Shops, trades, jobs and professions*), French does not use an indefinite article after the verbs **être** or **devenir**:

she is a captain	= **elle est capitaine**
David is a sergeant	= **David est sergent**
they are hoping to become corporals	= **ils espèrent devenir caporaux**

French also omits the article in the following:

to be promoted (to) major	= **être promu commandant**

and (as usual) in constructions with **de**:

to have the rank of lieutenant	= **avoir le rang de lieutenant**

But if an adjective is introduced, the indefinite article is obligatory and **il(s)/elle(s)** are replaced by **ce**:

he's a British general	= **c'est un général britannique**
they are French colonels	= **ce sont des colonels français**

When referring to people, use their rank preceded by **le** (note lower-case initial letter when written):

Colonel Smith has arrived	= **le colonel Smith est arrivé**
ask Sergeant Dubarry	= **demandez au sergent Dubarry**

When speaking directly to people, do not use expressions with **mon**. These are only used within the French army by inferiors speaking to superiors. Anyone else should use the rank as a title without **mon**:

| yes, Captain | = **oui, capitaine** |
| good morning, Admiral | = **bonjour, amiral** |

See also *Forms of address*.

....

Meals

Here are some names of meals:

breakfast	= **petit déjeuner** *m*
dinner	= **dîner** *m*
lunch	= **déjeuner** *m*
supper	= **souper** *m*

Note, in the following examples, that French sometimes hesitates, especially with **dîner** and **déjeuner**, between the noun with **le**, and the verb. This is because the words **déjeuner**, **dîner** and **souper** are both nouns (*lunch, dinner, supper*) and verbs (*to lunch, to dine, to sup*).

Translating *to*

The verb form is preferred:

| I'm not having them to lunch again | = **je ne les inviterai plus à déjeuner** |
| guess who's coming to dinner | = **devine qui vient dîner** |

Translating *for*

There are two possibilities here:

| who have you invited for dinner? | = **qui as-tu invité à dîner?** (*verb*) |
| what did you have for lunch? | = **qu'est-ce que tu as mangé au** (*or* **pour**) **déjeuner?** (*noun*) |

Translating *over*

pendant is the preferred translation and requires the 'article + noun' form:

let's discuss it over dinner	= **discutons-en pendant le dîner**
the business was concluded over breakfast	= **l'affaire a été conclue pendant le petit déjeuner**
they fell in love over a business lunch	= **ils sont tombés amoureux pendant un déjeuner d'affaires**

Translating *at* **(+ time)**

pour is used for the future and **pendant** in other cases:

I'll see you at lunch time	= **on se voit pour (le) déjeuner**
at breakfast, she announced that...	= **pendant le petit déjeuner, elle a annoncé que...**

Adjective and adverb

Where English uses 'adjective + noun', French often prefers 'verb + adverb':

to have an early/a late lunch	= **déjeuner tôt/tard**
to eat a hearty dinner	= **bien dîner**

The verb form is also preferable in:

to give the dog its dinner	= **donner à manger au chien**

And **déjeuner/dîner** are avoided in the following:

to go out to lunch/dinner	= **sortir** (*or* **aller**) **au restaurant à midi/le soir**

English compounds are often translated by French expressions with **de**, often followed by the definite article:

the lunch menu	= **le menu du déjeuner**
dinner time	= **l'heure du dîner**

But this is an area where French and English often
express things in quite different ways:

the breakfast room	=	**la petite salle à manger**
a dinner party	=	(*simply*) **un dîner**
a dinner plate	=	**une grande assiette**

....

The human voice

Here are the names of the principal voices. Note that it is
sometimes necessary to distinguish the word for the
voice from that for the singer. This can also involve a
change of gender.

	Voice	Singer
soprano	**soprano** *m*	**soprano** *m* or *f* (depending on whether boy soprano or woman)
mezzo-soprano	**mezzo-soprano** *m*	**mezzo-soprano** *f*
contralto	**contralto** *m*	**contralto** *f*
alto	**alto** *m*	**alto** *m*
counter-tenor	**haute-contre** *f*	**haute-contre** *m*
tenor	**ténor** *m*	**ténor** *m*
baritone	**baryton** *m*	**baryton** *m*
bass-baritone	**baryton-basse** *m*	**baryton-basse** *m*
bass	**basse** *f*	**basse** *f*

Article or no article?

The constructions to use are similar to those for
professions (see *Shops, trades, jobs and professions*):

he's a tenor	=	**c'est un ténor** *or* **il est ténor**
he sings tenor	=	**il chante ténor**

Gender of singer or voice?

Because of possible 'clashes' between the genders of

words and the sex of people, one may need to prefer one
construction to another:

he's a bass	= **c'est une basse** *or* **il a une voix de basse**
she's an alto	= **c'est un alto** *or* **elle a une voix d'alto**

Translating English compounds:

Note that there is no **de** in:

the tenor part	= **la partie ténor**

But there is a **de** in:

a tenor solo	= **un solo de ténor**
a tenor voice	= **une voix de ténor**

....

Musical instruments

Here are the names of some common instruments:

bassoon	= **basson** *m*
cello	= **violoncelle** *m*
clarinet	= **clarinette** *f*
drum	= **tambour** *m* (*but* drums = **batterie** *f*)
flute	= **flûte** *f*
guitar	= **guitare** *f*
horn/French horn	= **cor** *m*
keyboard(s)	= **synthétiseur** *m*
oboe	= **hautbois** *m*
saxophone	= **saxophone** *m*
trombone	= **trombone** *m*
trumpet	= **trompette** *f*
viola	= **alto** *m*
violin	= **violon** *m*

Groups

the brass	= **les cuivres** *mpl*
the percussion	= **les percussions** *fpl*
the strings	= **les instruments** *mpl* **à cordes** *or* **les cordes** *fpl*
the wind	= **les instruments** *mpl* **à vent** *or* **les vents** *mpl*
the woodwind	= **les bois** *mpl*
duo	= **duo** *m*
trio	= **trio** *m*
quartet	= **quatuor** *m*
quintet	= **quintette** *m*
sextet	= **sextuor** *m*
septet	= **septuor** *m*
octet	= **octuor** *m*

Play

Note the use of **de** + definite article with **jouer** (as opposed to **à** when speaking of sports):

to play the violin	= **jouer du violon**
to play the trumpet	= **jouer de la trompette**

But note the use of **le** with **apprendre**:

to learn the piano	= **apprendre le piano**

Players

With French words ending in **-iste** the gender reflects the sex of the person:

he's a violinist	= **c'est un violoniste**
she's a violinist	= **c'est une violoniste**

It is always safe to use **joueur/joueuse de**:

a piccolo player	= **un joueur/une joueuse de piccolo**
a banjo player	= **un joueur/une joueuse de banjo**

Where English qualifies the word for a player with words
like *good, bad*, French prefers to use the verb **jouer** with
an adverb:

he's a good flautist	= **c'est un bon flûtiste** *or* **il joue bien de la flûte**
I'm a very bad pianist	= **je suis un très mauvais pianiste** *or* **je joue très mal du piano**

Like English, French can use the name of the instrument
to refer to the player:

she's a first violin	= **elle est premier violon**
not so loud, trumpets!	= **pas si fort, les trompettes!**

Translating English compound expressions

Where English has a compound expression, French
usually uses a term with **de**:

piano lessons	= **des leçons de piano**
a violin solo	= **un solo de violon**
a guitar teacher	= **un professeur de guitare**

But note the use of **à** when the term expresses purpose:

a violin case	= **un étui à violon**

French also uses **à** when referring to certain groups:

a string quartet	= **un quatuor à cordes**
a wind octet	= **un octuor à vent**

but:

a brass band	= **une fanfare**

And note the use of **pour** to indicate that a piece of music
is intended for a particular instrument:

a piano piece	= **un morceau pour piano**
an organ arrangement	= **un arrangement pour orgue**

a bassoon sonata	= **une sonate pour basson**
the viola part	= **la partie pour alto**

....

Dances

Here are some words for types of dances and dancing:

ballet	= **ballet** *m*
cha-cha	= **cha-cha-cha** *m*
dance	= **danse** *f*
minuet	= **menuet** *m*
rock and roll	= **rock** *m*
rumba	= **rumba** *f*
tango	= **tango** *m*
twist	= **twist** *m*
waltz	= **valse** *f*

In general, where English uses the name of the dance to express the action (verb), French uses **danser le/la X**:

she tangos beautifully	= **elle danse le tango magnifiquement bien**
to rock and roll the night away	= **passer la nuit à danser le rock**

Valser does exist as a verb, but is not always used:

he waltzes well	= **il valse bien** *or* **il danse bien la valse**
they waltzed round the room	= **ils ont fait le tour de la salle en dansant (la valse)**
he waltzed her round the room	= **il l'a entraînée dans une valse tout autour de la pièce**

Both languages refer to the dance form in the singular preceded by the definite article:

to do the rumba/tango	= **danser la rumba/le tango**
to teach the twist	= **enseigner le twist**

| to learn the tango | = | **apprendre le tango** |

Note the French use of the definite article in the following:

| to go to a dance | = | **aller au bal** |

Most English compounds are rendered by French expressions with **de**:

a dance band	=	**un orchestre de danse**
a rumba rhythm	=	**un rythme de rumba**
a waltz melody	=	**un air de valse**

Signs of the zodiac

Here are the signs of the Zodiac:

Aries	=	**le Bélier**
Taurus	=	**le Taureau**
Gemini	=	**les Gémeaux**
Cancer	=	**le Cancer**
Leo	=	**le Lion**
Virgo	=	**la Vierge**
Libra	=	**la Balance**
Scorpio	=	**le Scorpion**
Sagittarius	=	**le Sagittaire**
Capricorn	=	**le Capricorne**
Aquarius	=	**le Verseau**
Pisces	=	**les Poissons**

Use capital letters in French as in English.

When describing people, one frequently uses no article:

| I'm Leo | = | **je suis Lion** |

Other forms are possible, such as **de** + definite article:

I'm a Leo/born in Leo	= **je suis du Lion**
all my friends are Cancer	= **tous mes copains sont du Cancer**

And there are expressions using the indefinite article in both languages:

a typical Capricorn	= **un Capricorne typique**
to meet a Sagittarian	= **faire la connaissance d'un Sagittaire**

Where English has two forms, the name of the sign (which can be applied to people) and a noun/adjective, French usually has only one (and see below for rules for the use of plural **-s**):

they're Sagittarius or Sagittarians	= **ils sont Sagittaire**
she's Aquarius or an Aquarian	= **elle est Verseau**

The definite article is correct with both singular and plural (the latter being preferable), when describing people of a particular sign as a typical group:

Arians like that	= **le Bélier aime cela** or **les Bélier aiment cela**
Pisceans will feel the chill	= **il fera frisquet chez les Poissons** (*colloquial*)
what's the horoscope for Gemini?	= **que dit l'horoscope pour les Gémeaux?**

Note that, when referring to more than one person, no **-s** or **-x** is added in the plural, at least in normal practice (not always respected):

for Arians, Scorpios and Aquarians...	= **pour les Bélier, pour les Scorpion, pour les Verseau...**

But, vice versa, where the form is plural anyway, French naturally uses the plural form when referring to one person:

he is a Piscean	= **il est des Poissons**
she is Gemini	= **elle est Gémeaux**

When translating *in* a number of constructions are possible:

she was born in Scorpio *or* under the sign of Scorpio	= **elle est née sous le signe du Scorpion**
the sun is in Aquarius	= **le soleil est au Verseau**
the sun and Mercury in Gemini	= **le soleil et Mercure en Gémeaux**

Using Zodiac words as the first part of compounds

Often Zodiac names are treated like adjectives but with no agreement. Some of the following are typical of horoscope columns and might seem odd in general use. Try and avoid this area unless you are a professional!

a Leo woman/man	= **une femme Lion/un homme Lion**
a Pisces man won't surprise you	= **un homme Poissons ne va pas vous surprendre**
an Arian woman and a Taurean man (Fire and Earth) are two mammals who can't get on together	= **femme Bélier et homme Taureau (Feu et Terre), voilà deux mammifères qui ne peuvent pas s'entendre**
all your Scorpio characteristics	= **toutes vos caractéristiques Scorpion**
a Gemini temperament	= **un tempérament Gémeaux**
Libra ways of behaving	= **des comportements Balance**

Artefacts

Containers

Here are the names of some common containers:

bag	=	**sac** *m*
bowl	=	**bol** *m*
box	=	**boîte** *f*
can	=	**boîte** *f* **(de conserves, de bière,** *etc.***)**
case	=	**valise** *f*
cup	=	**tasse** *f*
jug	=	**carafe** *f*
pot	=	**pot** *m*
sack	=	**sac** *m*
tin	=	**boîte** *f* **(de conserves)**

Full and empty containers (the use of *de, à,* etc.)

French normally uses **de** to refer to the container when it is full. Those expressions may correspond to the English word with or without *-ful*.

a bowl of sugar	=	**un bol de sucre**
a cup of coffee	=	**une tasse de café**
a cupful of sugar	=	**une tasse de sucre**
a bag/bagful of potatoes	=	**un sac de pommes de terre**
a tin/tinful of tomatoes	=	**une boîte de tomates**
a caseful of toys	=	**une caisse de jouets**

Sometimes French has special words to refer to the amount contained:

a spoonful of syrup	=	**une cuillerée de sirop**
a handful of coffee beans	=	**une poignée de grains de café**

If in doubt, you can almost always say **un(e) plein(e) X de Y**, as in **une pleine cuillère**. Similarly, **un plein sac, une pleine valise, une pleine tasse, une pleine boîte, une pleine caisse**, etc.

French uses **à** to refer to some containers that have been designed for a special purpose and can thus be bought as such:

a tea cup	=	**une tasse à thé**
a pie dish	=	**un plat à tarte**
a tool box	=	**une boîte à outils**
a champagne bucket	=	**un seau à champagne**

This gives rise to the distinction between

a tea cup	=	**une tasse à thé**

and

a cup of tea	=	**une tasse de thé.**

But this distinction is not possible with all words, and sometimes only **de**, or only **à** is possible, whether the container is empty or full:

a wine bottle/bottle of wine	=	**une bouteille de vin**
a matchbox/a box of matches	=	**une boîte d'allumettes**
a tool box/a box of tools	=	**une boîte à outils**

Note that the names of containers are used in many other expressions where they are followed by complements other than the thing contained:

a sleeping bag	=	**un sac de couchage**
a mitre box	=	**une boîte à onglets**
a silencer	=	**un pot d'échappement**

etc.

The container for the contents

As in English, one can use the name of the container for the name of the contents in many cases:

pour me another glass	=	**tu me verses encore un verre?**
how much a case?	=	**c'est combien le cageot/la cagette?**
the boxes are $4	=	**c'est 4 dollars la boîte**

Selling and buying

to sell potatoes by the sack	=	**vendre des pommes de terre par sac**
delivered by the case	=	**livré par caisses**
it is £2 a case	=	**c'est 2 livres la caisse**
they are 60 p a sack	=	**elles font 60 pence le sac**

See also *Currencies and money*.

....

Tools and weapons

Here are the names of some common tools and weapons:

Tools

ax(e)	=	**hache** *f*
chain saw	=	**tronçonneuse** *f*
chisel	=	**ciseau** *m* **à bois**
drill	=	**perceuse** *f*
file	=	**lime** *f*
hammer	=	**marteau** *m*
hay fork	=	**fourche** *f*
knife	=	**couteau** *m*
saw	=	**scie** *f*
screwdriver	=	**tournevis** *m*
spade	=	**bêche** *f*
spanner	=	**clé** *f*

Weapons

arrow	=	**flèche** *f*

bow	=	**arc** *m*
field gun	=	**canon** *m*
machine gun	=	**mitrailleuse** *f*
pistol	=	**pistolet** *m*
revolver	=	**revolver** *m*
rifle	=	**carabine** *f*
sword	=	**épée** *f*
torpedo	=	**torpille** *f*

French does not normally use the name of the object as a verb. There are a few special verbs:

| to saw | = | **scier** |
| to dig | = | **bêcher** |

Often a general verb is used, followed by the name of the object introduced by **à la/au**:

| to drill a hole | = | **percer un trou à la perceuse** |
| to axe someone | = | **tuer quelqu'un à la hache** |

Similarly:

to mortar a position	=	**attaquer une position au mortier**
to sabre the prisoners	=	**tuer les prisonniers au sabre**
to bayonet the enemy	=	**tuer l'ennemi à la bayonnette**

This means that the same English expression can have several translations:

| to hammer down a wall | = | **casser un mur à coups de marteau** |
| to hammer down a lid | = | **fermer une caisse à coups de marteau** |

etc.

In some cases, the translation is unpredictable:

to knife	=	**donner un coup de couteau**
to be knifed	=	**recevoir un coup de couteau**
to shell the position	=	**bombarder le poste (à coups d'obus)**

Note the use of **de** where English has compounds:

a hammer blow	=	**un coup de marteau**
a gun shot	=	**un coup de fusil**

Boats and vehicles

Here are the names of some common boats and vehicles:

Boats and ships

catamaran	=	**catamaran** *m*
ferry	=	**ferry** *m*
freighter	=	**cargo** *m*
hovercraft	=	**aéroglisseur** *m*
liner	=	**paquebot** *m*
(oil) tanker	=	**pétrolier** *m*
rowing boat	=	**barque** *f*
yacht	=	**yacht** *m*

Vehicles

bicycle/bike	=	**vélo** *m or* **bicyclette** *f*
bus	=	**bus** *m or* **autobus** *m*
car	=	**voiture** *f or* **auto** *f or* **automobile** *f*
coach	=	**car** *m*
lorry/truck	=	**camion** *m*
motor-cycle/motorbike	=	**moto** *f or* **motocyclette** *f*
plane/airplane/ aeroplane	=	**avion** *m*
train	=	**train** *m*

en and *à*

Traditionally **en** is used for vehicles you sit or stand in and **à** for those you sit astride:

a crossing by ship	=	**une traversée en bateau/ferry**

I go to London by bus/by = **je vais à Londres en bus/en**
car/by plane/by   **voiture/en avion/en train**
train

they went to London on = **ils allèrent à Londres à cheval**
horseback

For some vehicles, both **à** and **en** are possible:

I go to the village by = **je vais au village à bicyclette/à**
bicycle/motorbike   **vélo/à moto** or **en bicyclette/en**
                      vélo/en moto

par

par is used where English has *by*, with vehicles having
regular schedules: **par le train, par le bus, par avion, par
bateau** (note that there is no definite article with **avion** or
bateau).

dispatched by boat = **expédié par bateau**

but:

by the nine o'clock boat = **par le bateau de 9 heures**

Of course, **par** is impossible with words like **vélo** or
cheval (*see above*).

on / into; off / out of

to get on(to) a bicycle/ = **monter à vélo/à cheval**
a horse

to get on(to)/off a bus = **monter dans un bus/descendre d'un**
                        bus

to get onto/off/down = **monter dans le train/descendre du**
from the train   **train**

to get off a bicycle/a = **descendre de vélo/de cheval**
horse

to board/get off a boat/ = **monter à bord d'un/descendre d'un**
plane   **bateau/avion**

to ride a bicycle/a horse = **faire du vélo/du cheval**

on

I'll read it on the plane = **je le lirai dans l'avion**

| he was arrested on the train | = | **il a été arrêté dans le train** |

Compounds

a bus-driver	=	**un chauffeur de bus**
a bus stop	=	**un arrêt de bus**
a goods train	=	**un train de marchandises**
do you have a train timetable?	=	**avez-vous les horaires des trains?**

Other expressions

| the bus runs once an hour | = | **il y a un bus toutes les heures** |
| what time is your train? | = | **à quelle heure est votre train?** |

Note:

| the Dover coach | = | **le car de Douvres** |

This may mean *from Dover* or *to Dover*. To avoid ambiguity, one can say **le car pour Douvres/le car à destination de Douvres,** *or* **le car en provenance de Douvres.**

-load

a carload of brats	=	**une voiture pleine de garnements**
a truckload of bricks	=	**un camion plein de briques**
a boatload of refugees	=	**un bateau plein de réfugiés**

See also *Containers*.

....

Furniture

Here are the names of some common pieces of furniture:

armchair	=	**fauteuil** *m*
bed	=	**lit** *m*
bookcase	=	**bibliothèque** *f*

chair	=	**chaise** *f*
cooker	=	**cuisinière** *f*
cupboard	=	**placard** *m*
desk	=	**bureau** *m*
dish-washer	=	**lave-vaisselle** *m*
freezer	=	**congélateur** *m*
fridge	=	**réfrigérateur** *m*/**frigo** *m*
sofa	=	**canapé** *m*/**sofa** *m*
table	=	**table** *f*

French sometimes uses prepositions that are different from the one you would expect:

to take sth out of the fridge	=	**prendre qch dans le réfrigérateur**
to take sth off the table	=	**prendre qch sur la table**
to put sth in the fridge	=	**mettre qch au frigo**
to lie in bed	=	**être au lit**
to go to bed/get into bed	=	**aller au lit**
to get up off the chair	=	**se lever (de la chaise)**

Note also:

to get out of bed	=	**se lever**